James Trow

A Trip to Manitoba

James Trow

A Trip to Manitoba

ISBN/EAN: 9783337148287

Printed in Europe, USA, Canada, Australia, Japan

Cover: Foto ©Andreas Hilbeck / pixelio.de

More available books at **www.hansebooks.com**

A TRIP

TO

MANITOBA.

BY JAMES TROW, M. P.

QUEBEC:

S. MARCOTTE, PRINTER & PUBLISHER,

—

1875.

PREFACE.

The following Letters addressed to the Editor of the *Stratford Beacon* by Mr. Trow, M. P. are reproduced as containing notes of travel over the Dawson route, and impressions of the Province of Manitoba with respect to its capabilities.

A TRIP TO MANITOBA.

—

LETTERS FROM MR. TROW, M.P.

—

(To THE EDITOR OF THE *Stratford Beacon*.)

DEAR SIR,—I ask you and the numerous readers of the
BEACON to excuse my delay in fulfilling my prom... o
furnish you weekly with sketches of my ramblings in   o
North West.   The only reasonable apology I am prepared
to offer is, the route to the head waters of Lake Superior
has been so often described by excursionists, that nothing
new could be presented of interest to your readers; and
beyond that point one is, comparatively speaking, shut
out from society for some weeks—no postal communication, and no facilities for writing, unless sitting in your
tent with a boulder for your writing desk could be dignified with the name of comfort.   At convenient intervals,
however, I took jottings by the way, and now embrace
the earliest favorable opportunity of presenting them to
the readers of the BEACON.

On the morning of the 9th of July, accompanied by two
of my sons, I wended my way to Shakespeare station.   On

the train, according to arrangement, we met our mutual friend, Mr. Wm. Davidson, Reeve of Fullarton, bound for Manitoba. In Toronto we overtook our "companion-in-arms," Mr. Thos. Matheson, Mayor of Mitchell, light-hearted and sociable, prepared for any emergency ; possessed of no care, being his own earthly adviser, and like a silk worm could wrap himself in his own garment ; live on land or sea, and if the chapter of accidents should land him beneath the waves of the great lakes, or make him fall a prey to the cruelty of the " untutored savage," he would leave no chasm in society, unless in the hearts of many fair damsels who have so long endeavored in vain to persuade him that a life of "single blessedness" was never intended by the Creator for His creatures. How different is the case of the married man ! His cares are legion. Before attempting to move, he must of necessity consult his " other self, " acquaint his family and his wife's relations ; and his banker must not be overlooked ; he has calls to make ; debts to meet ; funds to provide for himself and for the maintenance of his family during his absence ; may be chancery suits or possibly contested elections to watch ; should he, fortunately, happen to be, like the Treasurer of Ontario, the lucky possessor of a handsome surplus, some honest man must be found to invest or *squander* it for him during his absence. These and sundry other inconveniences obviated, I for one highly approve of people possessed of means

TAKING A SUMMER TRIP,

recruiting one's mental and physical energies by change of scenery, relaxation from business cares and inhaling the pure invigorating atmosphere ; and I know of no portion of this Dominion better adapted for the enjoyment of a few weeks than on our nothern lakes. There you can get a view of nature in its primeval simplicity.

Having secured our tickets, we left the Toronto Union station, which certainly is a misnomer, for evidently no unanimity among the various lines of railway exists. The trains of the Northern and great Western pass the Union Station east and west, and yet you are put to the expense and inconvenience of hiring a conveyance to remove your baggage from one station to another, returning upon the same track. Such a feeling should not exist. The different companies should work more harmoniously together. The public who pay for the construction of these great thoroughfares have rights which should be respected.

For the first 45 or 50 miles we pass through a beautifully rich, undulating country, embellished with substantial mansions, commodious barns and outhouses, orchards, ornamental trees and pleasure groves. Barrie is a beautiful town situated at the head of

LAKE SIMCOE,

on a gentle slope from the lake. The northern section of the Northern Railway runs through a new country, in many places low and marshy. The line is kept in good repair, under the able management of Col. Cumberland, M. P. P. The various station houses and surroundings are got up with considerable taste. Arrived at Collingwood, 94 miles from Toronto, on the Nottawasaga Bay, or southern point of the Georgian Bay, the usual bustle and confusion incident to lake travel was witnessed ; sobs and sighs, kissing and shaking of hands by parting friends. Some had forgotten trunks, others more trifling things. One aristocratic Englishman had left his poodle dog ashore, and our friend, Mr. Davidson, in marching across the deck, accidentally upset a cage containing a canary, which when set at liberty made a bee-line for the shore, to the great chagrin of the chambermaid, who made diligent inquiry for the culprit. Fortunately no person informed, or Fullarton would have lost the valuable services of the able reeve, for the irate Abigail appeared determined to throw some person overboard after her pet canary. Before passing Cabots Head, we sighted a wrecked steamer—the *Mary Ward*—on the rocks, probably a mile or more from shore. Eight lives were lost at the time of the disaster. Many unsuccessful attempts have been made to remove the wreck. During the night we passed Owen Sound, and before morning we encountered head winds. A tremendous lurch or two had the effect of bringing many on deck much earlier than they anticipated, and gave them an opportunity of seeing what they probably never saw before—the sun rising. Many strode the deck with a dignified step, anxious to show their good seamanship; but gradually the circle grew smaller by degrees and beautifully less, until only seven out of seventy answered to the breakfast call.

Passing lonely islands we arrive at the

STRAITS OF KILLARNEY,

a deep narrow passage cut by nature's hand through the solid rocks, and extending for 50 miles between the north shore and the Manitoulin, a most romantic place. Here many poor, half-starved Indians are seen peeping through their tents. I noticed nothing very remarkable in the village unless the sign over the only store in the place might be considered a curiosity. It read, "pay for all you purchase to-day, and get credit for all you want to-morrow." A good-sized hog that had learned the art of fishing, was "quite a learned pig." It could dive gracefully, and to all appearance often successfully.

During the following night we passed Cockburn and Drummond Islands and the Bruce Mines. These mines were formerly very productive, but the expense of transportation of the ore to Wales for smelting and refining proved unprofitable. Very few men are at present employed at the mines. Passing St. Joseph's and Sugar Islands, we enter Lake St. George, through which a narrow channel has been dredged. Passing Garden River settlement and numerous lovely little Islands, one of them is pointed out as the last resting place of the lamented Judge Prince, whose dying request was that his bones should be interred on the island, "and it was done accordingly." Early in the day we arrive at

SAULT ST. MARIE.

The village on the Canadian side is nicely located on the river, rising gradually to the rear, and contains probably 500 inhabitants, composed of whites, half-breeds and Indians; the latter employ themselves in fishing, and appear to hold an exclusive right of catching fish under the rapids. Like most Indians they are wretchedly clothed and fed. Crossing the river, in order to pass through the canal, we are delayed a short time, and taking a stroll through the town, visit Fort Brady, &c. This canal was completed in 1855; some 1,000 men were employed for nearly two years on the works, the contractors receiving 750,000 acres of land for the work. It is a little over a mile in length, width 115 feet, having two locks 350 feet in length; 70 feet at top; 25 feet high.

A MUCH LARGER CANAL

is now in course of construction alongside, having only one lock. I am informed that a canal can be constructed on the Canadian side of the river at much less expense, the distance being less than one half. A work of such vital importance to the trade and navigation of the Upper Lakes should be undertaken and completed, and the

Government not again be in the humiliating position of applying to Washington for a permit to pass the canal with munitions of war, as we were at that critical period of our history—the rebellion in the North West. Passing through the canal we enter the great inland sea, Lake Superior, the largest body of fresh water in the world, 460 miles in length, and 170 broad at its widest point. This Lake is subject to tides which, though faint, are perceptible, and sudden changes. Millions of tons of rocks and boulders, slime and sediment, have been scooped out and carried by the resistless glaciers or torrents and scattered promiscuously hundreds of miles south. The numerous cuts and rents through the rocky mountains, bluffs and peaks along the northern shore give ample testimony of the fearful torrents, and how many have resisted the desperate attacks of ice and floods, and still stand as monuments of past ages.

CLIMATIC EFFECTS.

These great inland seas, or large bodies of water, tend to ameliorate the climate. They are in fact great reservoirs of warmth. Frosts come later in the fall than further inland. Grapes and peaches grow luxuriantly in the county of Huron, adjoining the lakes, that will not grow in the county of Perth in the same latitude. Fall frosts do not injure the root crops in the counties of Grey and Bruce as much or as early as in more southern counties, evidently proving that large bodies of water retain heat and moderate the weather.

Shortly after leaving the canal, we arrived at Point Aux Pins, a long pine-clad shore with sandy beach. A little further we pass Cape Gros and Iroquois Tower, called the portals to Lake Superior. These points are rugged rocks stretching away in the distance. Steaming northwest some 70 miles, we arrive at

MICHIPICOTON ISLAND,

the gem of Lake Superior's deep waters. There is here a safe and commodious harbor, adorned at the entrance by a cluster of islands on which agates and other precious stones are found. From this point we pass through deep and capacious channels, bluffs and promontories, many rising abruptly hundreds of feet above the water, and in one or two instances over a thousand feet, clad with stunted trees. Red Rock, an old Hudson Bay station, is reported to be the best fishing ground on the north shore, and here several Americans left the boat to fish. The Hon. James Simpson and family intended spending a few weeks in the locality. Retracing our steps, we enter Lake Superior about daybreak, and speedily arrive at Silver Islet, a diminutive spot but containing the richest silver veins in the world, estimated to be worth millions of dollars; the original shares of $50 selling at $25,000. Leaving this Eldorado, we steam past Thunder Cape, 1350 feet high, enter the great Bay, 25 miles in length, by probably 15 in width, and crossing the Bay arrive at

PRINCE ARTHUR'S LANDING,

a town now of considerable importance, containing numerous good stores, commodious hotels and extensive places of business. The harbor seems too open and liable to heavy storms, particularly when the wind blows from the south and south east. I visited this place in 1868. It was then a barren waste, with only two or three shanties. It is now incorporated, and is a prosperous town.

Prior to leaving the steamship *Cumberland*, at the suggestion of many of the cabin passengers, resolutions complimenting Captain Parsons and officers for their courtesy and attention during the trip, were signed by all the passengers, and presented to the Captain. The steamer had scarcely touched the wharf, when Mr. M. M. Thompson, of the firm of Messrs. Carpenter & Co., Government contractors for conveying immigrants from Prince Arthur's Landing to Fort Garry, came on board, anxious to ascertain how many of the passengers intended passing over the

DAWSON ROUTE.

In the short space of one hour Mr. Thompson had made arrangements for removing westward all the passengers and their baggage. Our party concluded to remain a day and visit my old friend, Mr. Adam Oliver, M. P. P. for South Oxford, Mr. Wilson, custom house officer at Thunder Bay, volunteering to row us over some four miles to Fort William. Landing at the Fort, we enjoyed the hospitality of the Hudson's Bay agent. Mr. McIntyre, and his amiable lady. Mr. Oliver's mills, the nucleus of a second Chicago, are beautifully situated on the Kaministiquia river, some half a mile from its entrance into Thunder Bay. Mr. Oliver is in possession of some 35,000 or 40,000 acres of timber and farming land skirting the river, and running south almost to the United States boundary. The river is sluggish, very crooked, and navigable for 12 miles. Afterwards there is a succession of falls which impedes or entirely stop navigation. Mr. Oliver entertained our party to an excursion some distance up the river, past McKay's mountain, in his beautiful tug *Jennie Oliver*, returning to lunch, and afterwards across the bay to the Landing. With the assistance of Mr. Thompson, we made preparations for prosecuting our trip the following day, and having purchased a few luxuries that could not be procured at the stations on the route, we retired to rest, having accomplished a little over 700 miles of our trip.

I shall in my next confine my remarks to our trip from Prince Arthur's Landing, over the Dawson route, and entrance into Fort Garry.

Yours, &c.,

JAMES TROW.

DEAR SIR,—I concluded my last communication at Thunder Bay, or, properly speaking, Prince Arthur's Landing, a place now noted for its extraordinarily rapid growth, as well as for its silver interests. The very streets show veins of silver; prospecting being the prevalent topic. Speculation often runs wild. Mineral locations are sold for fabulous sums and resold repeatedly. One victim wants to victimize another. Either silver or gold may be purchased too dear. Considerable interest is now felt by the inhabitants of Prince Arthur's Landing in respect to the terminus of the Superior end of the great Pacific Railway. Many leading men in the town assert that the importance of the place will be a sufficient guarantee, and that the Government cannot overlook their claims. To me, as an impartial observer, totally disinterested, the harbor appears not by any means a safe one, exposed as it is to the whole sweep of storms from the lake, unless it is protected by breakwaters of considerable length, extending far out into the bay. Some advocate the mouth of the Kaministiquia river. I find that my friend, Mr. Adam Oliver, M. P. P., and Mr. McIntyre, Hudson Bay agent, are strongly in favor of this being the terminus.

THE KAMINISTIQUIA

is certainly sheltered from storms, but before large steamers could conveniently enter, very expensive dredging is requisite, both of the river and some distance into the bay. The *debris* brought down the river by floods for ages past blocks up the entrance, yet we find splendid harbours at Milwaukee and also at Chicago made out of former insignificant rivers. Some eminent surveyors and engineers are advocates of making Nepigon the terminus, being more in a direct line with this great thoroughfare, should the eastern section ever be constructed, and should our extensive lakes and rivers be utilized. They claim that Nepigon is much nearer the Sault, that this route is sheltered for 40 or 50 miles through the channel, that it is not exposed to the sweep of Lake Superior so much as Thunder Bay, and that with some widening of the curves and improving the rapids at the Red Rock and Lake Ellen, steamers of the largest size could enter Nepigon. The Government will unquestionably in the interest of the Dominion select the most eligible location.

Before leaving Prince Arthur's Landing, like all travellers and immigrants, we were interviewed by paid American agents, who took a deep interest in our welfare, urging upon our party not to risk our precious lives on the

DAWSON ROUTE;

that it was morally committing suicide to attempt to go any other way than by Duluth and across the Northern Pacific; that not less than 400 poor half-famished immigrants were then at the North West angle, and had been there for weeks; no teams, no provisions, perfect starvation prevailed, that if we persisted we might possibly get through before Christmas or New Year's but in all probability our bones would be left to bleach on some portage or sunk beneath the waves; that if we wished for comfort in travelling, combined with speed, by all means, take the American route; and providing we required land, the broad prairies were inviting us in Minnesota or Dacota. These smooth-tongued interlopers succeeded in poisoning the minds of several who intended to go through our own country. Agents of this kind are found in almost every city and town in the Dominion, seducing and influencing good settlers to cross the borders and swell the great Republic. Such things are common, and should no longer be tolerated. What would be your feelings, Mr. Editor, if half a dozen unscrupulous agents employed by a rival in business, were continually hanging around your counter, depreciating the value of your goods and praising those of your rival? And what appears to me most incredible, I am informed many Canadians are enlisted in this service, and like a certain American bird, are befouling their own nest and belittling their native country.

We left the landing the following morning for

SHEBANDOWAN,

45 miles by stage. For the first 16 miles the road is good, running round moderately sized hills mostly up grade. The soil is light; timber, poplar and white birch, tall but not heavy; the land is, in my opinion, equally as good as that in many parts of Wisconsin or Michigan, and decidedly preferable to many parts of Minnesota. We noticed wild fruit in abundance, and flowers of every hue; timothy seed, that had been sowed purposely or scattered by the way, growing luxuriantly. In three hours we arrived at the first station, located on the rising ground with a nice little lake in front. Some thirty teams, belonging to the contractors, were at this point either feeding or changing. From this station west for miles the soil is heavy clay, the road in a bad state of repair, but then undergoing improvements, the necessary

repairs on which were delayed owing to some misunderstanding in the terms of agreement. A distance of six miles further we cross the Kaministiquia, broad and rapid, spanned by a splendid wooden bridge. This point is 22 miles by land and 45 to the mouth of the river. Travelling six miles further we cross the river Mattawan, a considerable stream that flows from Lake Shebandowan. This river is also spanned by a permanent bridge alongside a lovely waterfall and rapids. We find a solitary settler located near the bridge who has made considerable clearing, raised good buildings and appears to be in the possession of all the elements of comfort. After crossing the Mattawan, which is a considerable stream, bordered with hills and bluffs and delightful scenery, we climb hills many hundreds of feet in height, cross some very rough and uneven corduroy bridges, and, what appears to a casual observer singular, many corduroy bridges are on the hill tops or the down grade, where ditches or drains would keep the road bed dry. The soil is light and sandy, intermixed with white clay and limestone, with here and there, white rock, the greater part of the way to Shebandowan, at which place we arrived early in the afternoon. This station is situated on the eastern borders of the lake. The buildings are good, and the station-master, Mr. Darby, very courteous and accommodating. We noticed considerable freight lying on the wharf, principally heavy merchandize and agricultural implements. The contractors were anxious to push through passengers with their provisions and clothing in advance of freight. We were accommodated with beds in the Government store, and were not under the necessity of pitching our tents. Early in the morning, the boats were laden almost to the water's edge. The steam-tug attached, we were again pushing our way at the rate of six or seven miles an hour on the bosom of this lovely sheet of water, passing on the way several islands thickly covered with verdure and evergreens. In less than four hours we arrived at

KASHABOIWE PORTAGE,

three-fourths of a mile in length. Before reaching this portage we met Mr. Dawson's canoe, paddled by six stalwart Indians and half breeds, skimming through the water at a high velocity, to meet their chief at the head waters of Lake Superior, he having gone to Fort Garry. Kashaboiwe Lake is a small sheet of water, and there being numerous narrows and windings the scenery is very pretty. The timber on the adjoining lands is much heavier than around Shebandowan. The next portage is called the "height of land," supposed to be one thousand feet above the level of lake Superior. We noticed several Indian camps, and squaws and papooses picking berries and the inner bark of the pine or spruce, which they chew incessantly. At the west end of the portage we enter Lac des Mille Lacs, probably the most picturesque lake in the whole route, studded as it is with innumerable islands, bays, headlands and channels, of every imaginable shape and form. The traveller is amazed how the navigator finds his way through such intricate windings. Next we arrive at Barrel Portage. Remaining at

BARREL STATION

overnight, we had our tents pitched on the hill-side, our bed being spruce and pine brush, with our satchels or a stone for a pillow; made a smudge fire at the opening, and fanned the smoke into the tent to clear away mosquitoes. After a scanty supper of bread, pork, molasses and beans, washed down with a boiled substitute for tea, we courted the embrace of Morpheus. Not having made calculations to fare sumptuously every day or be clothed in purple and fine linen, we were prepared to buffet the waves and bless heaven for all its dispensations. Entering our tent, not a mosquito dare show his face under that canvas. Our smudge fire had heated up the tent to an insufferable degree, and the smoke was absolutely suffocating; however, this was preferable to being bled and blistered by countless swarms of mosquitoes and sand flies. The former is a gentleman, and gives you timely notice of his approach, and confines his attacks principally to the face and hands, but the minute little flesh-color sand fly is impertinence personified. He will enter your stockings, crawl into your boots, up your trowsers, all over your person, take a bite here and there on his rambles, get on your head and face, and after a preliminary survey of you externally, crawl up your nostrils, into your ear, or down your throat, and examine you internally. I am by no means nervous, and I get credit for being calm and collected under difficulties, but I confess these rascally sand flies so provoked and exasperated me that I involuntarily conjugated a verb, or perhaps two, in the imperative mood. I confess, too, that I never had a greater desire to enjoy a trip heavenwards or return to Shakespeare—which is the next best place—than when under the surgical operations of these unmerciful mosquitoes and sand-flies at Barrel portage. Before daylight the smoke had cleared away and we were literally covered. The swarm had made a raid either through the keyhole or a rent in the canvas. Our fellow voyageur, the respected Mayor, good exemplary man, notwithstanding that like the prodigal son, he fared miserably, did not shrink away from his just proportions, but had absolutely increased in size during the night—about the gills! The Reeve looked as if he had been dragged through a brush heap, and had to acknowledge that notwithstanding his amiableness of temper, the torment was almost beyond endurance. But after a vigorous siege, a truce was held, and the enemy withdrew. After getting a wash and prying open our eyelids, we observed on the bare ground a poor Indian and squaw and several children, with only a miserable blanket to cover their nakedness, and with, to all appearance, nothing in store for their morning's meal. The Indian mode of living is very precarious. Possessed of no forethought, the red man makes no provision for the future. It is either shameful waste, when he has plenty, or semi-starvation. We left this station at early dawn and wended our way down the narrows to

LAKE WINDIGOOSTIGAN,

and in a few hours crossed with the steam tug to French Portage, a distance of 12 miles. Teams and waggons are at all portages of any size, to convey passengers and freight across. Our party, anxious to know if their limbs were useful members of the body corporate, preferred walking, the Mayor leading the way, singing "O be joyful." Considerable baggage had accumulated at the west end of the portage, and the men stationed for that work appeared very indifferent about the interests of the travelling community. One Englishman said he would sooner be hanged in England than die a natural death on the Dawson Route. The freight was all helter skelter about the landing, and no wood having been prepared for the tug, necessitated our remaining two or three hours. I noticed a good-sized barge on the stocks, two-thirds finished, and also the log framework of new station buildings, the timber for which is all sawed by hand—certainly a slow and expensive process. This portage is a bed of sand and rock, the land being worthless. Our next lake was Kaogassikok, the shores of which are lined with scrub, pine and spruce with a sprinkling of larch and cedar. The damming of the outlets raises the water in many of these lakes several feet higher than their natural level. We arrived at the

ISLAND OF PINES

for dinner, and again partook of the bounties of life—
pork, bread and beans. Did eating by proxy serve the
purposes of nature, I would willingly have assigned my
right, title and interest, in every dainty dish for a trifle.
Crossing a small portage we came to a little lake, and
were rowed across some 9 miles. On the rising ground
near the landing we noticed several Indian camps. One
large tent was pointed out to us as being the residence
of the great chief or orator, Blackstone, who rules su-
preme, having some eighty warriors under his control,
and three wives. The wives prepare all the fuel as well
as food, pack and unpack tents when moving, carry the
tents and blankets, dress the skins of animals; in fact,
do all the work. While the boat was preparing for the
start, Blackstone made his appearance, accompanied by
his aged father, an old man with a villainous countenance.
I presented father and son with a few cigars, for which
they appeared thankful. Blackstone has fine chiselled
features, and a wild and cunning eye. It is alleged that
he was a leading spirit in the Minnesota massacre, 12
years ago, when not less than 1600 defenceless, harmless
settlers, men, women, and children, were mercilessly
butchered in cold blood. Crossing

STURGEON LAKE,

some 22 miles, a beautiful star-light night, the engineer
put on all steam, the fresh fuel causing a continual shower
of sparks to play around, the moon shining upon the
silvery lake. Passing alongside islands, and running
narrows, in some places so narrow that the hindmost boat
would swing against the land, the entire scene was particularly weird and romantic. Late at night we arrived
at Malyne Portage or rapids. The natives are numerous

at this point. The station buildings are rough log shanties. Across the river we noticed the Hudson Bay store, where supplies are usually kept to trade with the Indians for furs. Our tent having been pitched on the brow of a precipitous rock by the company's employees, and the night cold and chilly, we invited a few friends to our "castle in the air" to smoke a good cigar and imbibe a small decoction of Hennessy's best. With considerable dignity I ordered my son to unpack and bring forth the beverage, but judge of our astonishment, when we discovered the box well secured but the contents missing! Early next morning we prepared to shoot the

MALYNE RAPIDS.

These are miserably rocky rapids, but we made a safe descent. This section is very rough, of a primitive formation, granite rocks broken and torn, with very scanty vegetation. The river near the rapids widens and runs smoothly, after which its velocity increases, and eddies are formed. The waters seem loath to make the plunge, but are forced forward by the current behind. The excitement is great. Passing over these seething waters, the head man is at the bow with a strong paddle, the rest at their posts. The oarsmen are at work, and as swift as an arrow the boat shoots down and gets into the smooth waters below, where a small steamer, *Lilly of the West*, is waiting to pick up our boats. Many get washed by the spray, and in some instances the boats are upset and dashed upon the rocks, but with experienced men there is no danger. Passing down the rapids and crossing Lac La Croix, some thirty miles, we arrive at Pemmican Portage, where I shall for the present take leave of you and my readers.

I promised in my last letter to carry the reader through to Fort Garry, but by so doing this letter would reach an unreasonable length. Next week I shall resume our ramblings from this point to Fort Garry.

Yours truly,

JAMES TROW.

DEAR SIR,—In my last communication I noticed our arrival at Pemmican Portage. The baggage and passengers were immediately taken ashore, and teams and carriages were in waiting to carry us across to the steamer at the west end, distant four and a half miles. Considerable freight and passengers' baggage were at the landing for shipment, and it became necessary for all the masculines not afflicted with the gout, or who had not cork legs, or no legs at all, to walk. The softer sex, and all juveniles, were allowed to ride; myself and the mayor (in order to keep our dignity) perched ourselves upon the uppermost tier of boxes, so that we might get a Pisgah view of the surrounding country. Our teamster having previously received instructions to travel at a high velocity to catch the boat, paid no attention to our cries and lamentations. We held on like grim death; we dare not for a moment let go to brush the musquitoes from our faces, and endured this torture for 4½ miles, across the roughest corduroy and rocks in Christendom. Judge of our disappointment and chagrin on reaching the west end of the portage, to find that our express had arrived five minutes late; the steamer was seen winding its way around the island at the mouth to the bay. We then had no alternative but to retrace our steps, 4½ miles to the starting point, and remain over Sunday, but we took the precaution to walk back, having no desire to undergo a second infliction of being churned into a jelly. We pitched our tent and gracefully submitted to our fate, and partook of our frugal meal with considerable relish, having discovered that a little manual exercise was beneficial. After tea we took some exercise in paddling in canoes, finishing up with a good bath. Continuing our perambulations through the Indian village, we could see the natives peeping out through their tents with the eyes of terriers watching rats. Many were almost in a nude state, under no restraint and with no regard for decency.

After dark we received an invitation to

AN INDIAN POW-WOW

or dance, of which amusement the natives are passionately fond. We accepted the invitation. The ball took place in the largest tent, which was made of poles some 20 feet long, set up in a circular form, the small ends at the top, the large ends sufficiently spread out to give a large area at the base. This frame work was covered with birch bark, strips of blanket, skins or canvas. A fire was made in the centre of the tent, round which the noble savages danced. They formed a circle with their backs to the fire, joined hands, moved their feet up and down, beating time, and always marching round the circle singing "hi hi," or "he he." The old men and women lie on their backs, violently beating a tom-tom or tambourine, lacking the jingles. These children of nature must have practised their favorite steps upon heated plates of iron, for the same monotonous step and song continued from the beginning to the conclusion of the festivities. After gratifying our curiosity, we replenished the fire at our tent and retired to rest. The rotten dry limbs crackled so much and threw out such a glare of light that we often fancied our tent was on fire. The nights were exceedingly cold, and, as we had not taken the precaution of furnishing ourselves with a sufficiency of blankets, it was necessary to keep up the fires during the night. Early on Sunday morning we were called to partake of the bounties of life, pork, bread and beans, with a mongrel composition sacrilegiously called tea—boiled from the rising of the sun, taken out of the pot with a tin dipper, with more leaves than liquid, and flavored with West India molasses. After breakfast we had the satisfaction of seeing an Indian taking a steam bath, in which the tribe seem to have great faith. The bath-room is made of poles inserted in the ground, forming an arch, which is covered with bark, blanket, or skins. Inside are placed a number of hot stones, on which water is poured. The patient is put in naked and remains there till profuse perspiration is produced. Sometimes after coming out he plunges into cold water, and it is reported that some extraordinary cures are effected in this way.

A SAVAGE ON THE WAR PATH.

We spent the day roaming through the Indian encampments, often unthinkingly squatting down inside a tent, till cautioned by the station-master that the tents were literally crawling with vermin. However, we fortunately escaped without serious consequences. I noticed all day one elderly native, with high cheek bones, having a blue remnant of a blanket placed loosely over his loins, the upper part of the body bare, roaming from place to place. He held in his hand a large butcher knife, which he sharpened on a boulder. Occasionally he would look across the bay, and should a canoe come in sight, which many did during the day, he would lie crouched on the rock till it was sufficiently near for him to distinguish who were its occupants. Then he would jump up, and mutter the word "Chippawa," satisfied they were his own people and friendly. I watched his creeping, cautious movements, and I fancied that if the canoe contained a Sioux, his top knot would speedily be dangling at his belt.

The evening and night being warmer, the mosquitoes assembled in battalions, and being no respectors of official dignity, made a gallant attack upon the reeve and the mayor, who drew their heads into their trunks like mud-turtles, thrust their hands into their pockets, and slept soundly. Next morning the engineer and Mr. Devue, with six seamen, agreed to row us across to

KETTLE FALLS,

some 50 miles. Retracing our steps across this tedious portage, the boat was laden to the water's edge with freight. Many of the passengers enjoyed themselves sleeping, while the men were using every exertion to carry us to our destination. We made capital speed against head winds, across a large bay, some 12 miles, entered a channel and landed on a beautiful island. Here we made a fire, and cooked our meal, gathering berries for dessert. The fire spread almost instantaneously in every direction, and in all probability would burn for days or perhaps weeks. Again embarking, we rowed for some hours, and crossed a small portage of 20 rods in length, dragging our boat across logs and rocks, then launched again, reloaded and proceeded on our way. In a short time we came to another and much longer portage, which was passed in the short space of 20 minutes. Proceeding on our way, we crossed a lake of considerable dimensions, deviating from the route taken by the steamer. We passed through low marshy flats, that will in time be good meadow lands, the growth and decay of vegetation filling up and encroaching annually upon the water. At 5 o'clock in the evening we landed at Kettle Falls, one of the most comfortable and pleasant places on the route. A short distance above the falls the river is divided by an Island into two streams, on which are beautiful waterfalls or cascades, just above its entrance into Rainy Lake. At this portage we found a large gathering of Indians, much cleaner and more respectable looking than any we had seen on the route. Many of them were in the employ of the contractors, chopping wood and repairing a tramroad across the portage. Some were engaged in fishing and were apparently very successful. Splendid fish are caught under the falls. My son threw a trawl a few rods into the river, standing on shore, and dragging towards him, was successful almost every time in catching fish weighing from two to three pounds each. The Indians are inveterate consumers of the fragrant weed, and have no delicacy in begging tobacco. I purchased at a store in the place some of the coveted article and gave each a plug, for which they felt grateful. They mix it with a weed or plant they grow, called kinnekanik. Families often smoke in a circle, out of the same pipe, the head of the family or principal taking the first whiff and handing the pipe to the next, till it gets around the circle. Next time the leader takes two or three whiffs, and so it goes around. The pipe is made of black stone, often curiously carved, with much labour and ingenuity. This station was for some time kept by Mr. Uberhorst, of Downie, who put up good station buildings, and brought a nice patch of land under good cultivation. Timber in this locality is of good growth, and there are large tracts of land, apparently fit for cultivation and the production of crops. The falls are named from the numerous holes, resembling kettles, scooped out of the solid flat rocks of red sand stone. The following day we took a boat down the bay, around the island, and landed to examine the falls on the west channel. Between the Province and Minnesota these falls are grand beyond description ; the river is wide and deep. The seething waters plunge over the rocks, probably 35, feet perpendicularly. In one place many great chasms are cut or scooped out of the solid rocks and boulders, the size of a good house, are scattered about promiscuously. On the point of a precipice or rocky promontory, we noticed

AN INDIAN BURYING GROUND.

The bodies are wrapped up in bark, or in the canoe of the deceased, and placed upon stakes, probably eight feet above the surface of the ground, sufficiently high to protect the corpse from ravenous beasts. The friends of the deceased often examine and view the bones. Through the influence of the chief engineer and the kindness of Captain Cameron, who consented to start his boat at two in the morning, instead of ten the same day, we were enabled to connect with the steamer, leaving Fort Francis at ten, the hour that Captain Cameron's regulations were to leave Kettle Falls. Rainy Lake is upwards of 50 miles in length, which distance we had to make to connect with the boat. We found Captain Cameron a perfect gentleman, who did everything in his power to make the passengers comfortable. About 8 o'clock we sighted a raft, the men on board of which hailed us, anxious to be towed to Foster's mills at Fort Francis, but the Captain was determined to make connection, and declined giving them any assistance. Some two or three miles above the Fort the lake ends, and the passengers and baggage are put into boats and rowed down to within a quarter of a mile of the Fort. We had several horses on board and the steamer drawing too much water, anchored some 50 rods from shore. Ropes were put around the necks of the horses, when they were dragged or pushed overboard, and left to swim to land. As we approached

FORT FRANCIS,

evident signs of industry became more apparent. Numerous wigwams were standing on the plateau above the river. The Hudson Bay store and fort were substantial structures of wood. Many laborers are employed by the company, and also by Mr. Foster, who is constructing a steam mill at the Chaudière. The river at the falls is fully 200 yards wide, giving very extensive water power. We noticed one or two tolerably good gardens and considerable land around the Fort under cultivation. This station appears to be a general rendezvous for the natives, their usual feasts or celebrations being held in the locality. A dog feast had been recently held, which accounted for such a gathering. The Ojibbeways are a scattered tribe, much disorganized and roam about like gipsies. They are possessed of no forethought, make no provision for winter, and many die from absolute starvation. We had but little time at our disposal to view the Fort and surroundings. The steam tug being in readiness, with seven barges or boats strung behind, we presented addresses to the chief engineer, Mr Cowie, and to Captain Cameron, for their kindness, and started down this lovely river, which is scarcely noticed upon the map. Rainy river is almost uniform in width, and runs with an easy current through rich alluvial soil. The river banks are not high, but show evident traces that the bed has been much higher. The usual width of the river is probably half a mile, and the waters are turbid, owing to the loose nature of the soil, which continually keeps sliding and washing in its banks, although not so much on Rainy river as on the Red river. The banks are covered with grass and underwood, of such rank growth, that if luxuriant vegetation indicates rich soil, then the lands adjoining Rainy river must be rich indeed. Some 35 miles from Fort Francis we ran the

MANITOU RAPIDS.

These falls, with the scenery around, have much to charm and interest. The velocity of the water after turning a bend in the river is much increased, eddies being formed. We were carried along, plunging forward at great speed. Our boats should have been separated, but the tow was not loose, and the consequence was that three boats were caught by the eddy and carried back a considerable distance. We expected a similar fate, but our headsman cut the rope and we rushed down the river. These rapids, and also the Sault, some five miles further down, are formed by loose boulders, which could be removed without very much cost, and the river made navigable for steamers. The opportunities in this neighbourhood for water power are almost unequalled. The country around, as far as the eye can reach, is certainly fertile, and I am fully persuaded that the period is not far distant when we may find a busy and enterprising population utilizing these waters and cultivating their rich bottom lands. I noticed splendid corn and potatoes in this neighbourhood. And I could not help thinking that if the thousands of poor people who are undergoing partial starvation and hunger in many of the overcrowded cities of Europe, were located there, how happy and comfortable they might be.

RELICS OF PAST AGES.

Near the Sault, we noticed two very large mounds, and some smaller ones. These mounds are of different shapes, some round, others conical, and are supposed to be the graves of leading warriors of unknown generations. It is evident the work is artificial; it may have been constructed for burying the dead, or for protection against the inroads of invaders. The horses and as many of the passengers as preferred walking were landed at the wharf above Manitou falls ; those who wished to retain their seats and shoot the rapids remaining in the boats, the forces again uniting at the Sault station. Before landing, we were overtaken by a dreadful storm. The rain poured in torrents, the thunder roared continuously, and the lightning was terrific. Many were drenched to the skin, and must have been very uncomfortable.

My next letter will contain the account of our perambulations to Fort Garry.

Yours, &c.,

JAMES TROW.

—————

DEAR SIR.—In my last communication I left your readers at the Sault Rapids, Rainy River, where we had just landed in the face of a terrific storm. To our astonishment we discovered that this was a mere landing place at the head of present navigation, for large steamers plying from this point to the North West Angle. Here we found a vacant log house intended for temporary shelter for immigrants. The stationmaster, Mr. James Canniff, formerly of Belleville, a brother of the celebrated Dr. Canniff, of Toronto, assisted to provide for the ladies and their families, the male population being allowed to shift for themselves. Those of the passengers who had their own provisions, (and luckily all but ourselves were so provided), after the storm had abated, kindled fires, put on their pots and pans, and partook of their frugal fare. Our party had not been equally provident, having depended entirely for our supplies on the various stations *en route*. Mr. Canniff, worthy man, tried to console us by stating that the steamer must soon arrive and that we might expect sumptuous fare on board. However, hours passed and no signs of the craft.

MAKING A VIRTUE OF NECESSITY.

The Mayor gave a significant shake of the head, re-marking that our troubles were only commencing, and the Reeve resignedly observed that all was for the best, as the wife said when her husband broke his neck. We were not in the humor to "put on airs," but felt as hum-ble as whipped spaniels, and more like demolishing a plum pudding of large dimensions than living on the savory odor arising from the dainties of others. We were about retiring to our tent, in a resigned, philosophical mood, supperless, consoling ourselves that upon such frugal fare we would never be afflicted with the gout, and were prepared to endure with patience what could not be avoided, when Mr. Canniff remarked that it was very doubtful if the boat would attempt to come up the river till daylight, and that he would share with us his last morsel. We accepted his kind hospitality, and found in our entertainer a perfect gentleman. After an hour's con-versation, we retired for the night, and slept soundly after the hardships of the previous day. The Mayor rose early, with a good healthy complexion, a clear conscience, and satisfaction beaming on his contenance. The stea-mer was at the landing and we had every prospect of a good breakfast. We found Messrs. Carpenter and McGuin-nes, two of the contractors, on board, making prepara-tions to forward the passengers on their way. The storm accounted for the steamer's delay. Lake of the Woods is very shallow, its waters are easily ruffled and become exceedingly dangerous to navigate, more particularly near the mouth of Rainy River where there are beds of moving sand and sand bars, which obstruct the channel; and in the absence of any lighthouse—which is much needed—great caution is necessary.

DIFFICULTIES OF THE CONTRACTORS.

The contractors had moved every passenger from the North-West angle. An unusual rush of immigrants took them by surprise. The contract had been let so late in the season—about the middle of May and having found the barges and tugs greatly out of repair, the contractors had to provide so many horses, carriages, men and provisions, and move them from one point to another. This work occupied considerable time, and no doubt passengers were not made as comfortable or pushed forward with such speed as they would otherwise have been. Scores of Indians who were engaged in preparing fuel for the boats and stations had also to be provided with pork and flour. The contractors naturally calculated that the Indians could purchase provisions at the Hudson Bay stores, but they found that an Indian would not work for money, did not know its value, and would sooner have a pound of pork than a dollar bill. Providing for the men and their teams occupied a large portion of their carrying capacity, and the consequence was a general rush of immigrants, at the outset ; and to crown all, one Mr. Rolston who gave no intimation of his colony moving, landed at Prince Arthur's landing from Marquette, Michigan, with some 300 people. The contractors were unable to do more than they accomplished. Providing they get the contract for another season they could make much better preparations —have hay, oats, and wood, all upon the ground before navigation opens, the hands previously engaged, and the whole machinery in good working order. Mr. Carpenter was then travelling eastward to facilitate matters. Mr. McGuinnes returned with the boat to the North-West angle. The passengers and baggage being all placed on board, we again floated down this lovely river. Occasionally we saw a solitary settler, more frequently on the Minnesota side. We took in a quantity of wood piled on the river banks, purchased from the Hon. James McKay, who is the possessor of some miles of excellent timber bordering on the river, which is cut by Indians or half breeds for 80 cts. and sold for $2.50 per cord to the steamboat contractors. In six hours we passed Hungry Hall, a post of the Hudson Bay Company. We noticed many of the natives assembled on the banks of the river, who saluted us in the usual way, "bon jour." Before entering

LAKE OF THE WOODS,

we pass through low sedge or marshes apparently filling up, which will through time become extensive meadow lands: the encroached vegetable mould fringing and overlapping annually forms deposits, and narrows the water limits. We steamed straight across the lake for the angle, on our route passing several islets, some having verdure, others barren and naked, composed of primitive rocks or "old red sandstone." Occasionally you see streaks of mica slate. The different formations are thrown roughly together, some vertical, others flat. On one of these barren rocks we saw probably 60 or 80 tents, evidently a gathering of the natives for a dog feast or some other celebration, for there was no fuel on the island further than what they had taken with them in their small canoes. As we approached the angle the waters became more shallow. At last we cast anchor and were taken ashore in barges hauled by a small tug. The little river leading up to the landing was literally covered with canoes, the natives being evidently bent on sport. One fascinating, copper colored damsel seemed bent on trying a race with the tug, and skimmed over the water with great speed. The Reeve and myself were anxious to get the Mayor introduced to this lovely creature of the forest, but he was proof against the softer passions, and declined. The landing is on the American side, though far north of the 49th degree of latitude, brought about by some unaccountable diplomatic bunder. We wended our way into the station house, partook of a good meal, and made immediate preparations for continuing our journey by land carriage some 110 miles to

FORT GARRY.

After tea, our friend, Mr. McGuinnes, advised us to proceed immediately on our way and get to the first station, distant 16 miles, that night. We found at the door a four horse team hitched to a three-seated carriage with our baggage already loaded, and we proceeded over rough corduroy swamp and low marsh land at a good speed, with our heads envelopped in mosquito nets. About 12 o'clock at night we arrived at the station, in which we found three or four spans of horses, and the drivers asleep. In the centre was a roaring fire. Being dark, and not having a lantern, we preferred reclining in the shanty to pitching our tent, and slept comfortably. Making an early start we arrived at a comfortable station for breakfast, kept by an old acquaintance, Peter Pouli, of Downie, who made extraordinary preparations and gave us a good " square meal." From this point to

WHITE MUD RIVER.

the land is covered with tolerably-sized timber, very useful for railway ties, bridges or for building purposes ; but the land is loose and sandy, not fit for agricultural purposes. Yet I found many settlers located in Minnesota between Moorhead and Duluth on similar land. This station is kept by one McLeod, a Highland Scotchman, and his wife, who keep everything clean and comfortable, cultivating their own vegetables &c. They seemed to be enjoying the comforts of life. We overtook many immigrants at this point, with whom we conversed, several of them being from the counties of Huron, Bruce and Oxford. From here to Breakneck station, the road is good and large sums must have been expended before they were made passable. In many places we noticed hundreds of acres of timber burned down, the black charred stumps having a desolate appearance. A second growth soon shoots up, and what appears remarkable, should a growth of pine be destroyed by fire, the next crop may be oak, poplar or birch. The germs seem to exist in the soil, and have laid dormant probably for centuries. Perennial grasses and the first growth of timber appear to have an exclusive foothold until broken up with fire or cultivation. (I noticed when the Grand Trunk Railway was in course of construction, near extensive cuttings or excavations, that Canada thistles and other noxious weeds would spring up on this subsoil in localities where none were ever seen for miles before.) Towards night we arrived at

BREAKNECK STATION,

a wretched hovel, kept by a queer specimen of the *genus homo*. After some effort, we managed to bolt some half-cooked pork and dough cakes, promiscuously thrown together on the table, without any order or taste. The same ingredients could have been made palatable and acceptable with a little attention. This appears to be a general rendez-vous for flies. We were all unmercifully tortured during the night. The rest of the road, through beautiful natural groves to Oak Point, is good. About noon we emerged into a broad open prairie, the first on the route. Away in the distance, hundreds of cattle and horses were seen grazing on the open plain, and large fields of grain are waving in the wind. The outskirts of this grand panorama are dotted over with comfortable homesteads along the river Seine, which winds its tortuous course through a rich fertile country and empties its waters into the Red River near Winnipeg. Crossing the north-east angle of the prairie, we arrive at Oak Point, or more commonly called Prairie du Chien, the nucleus of a thriving village, adjoining the river, and containing a commodious store with a general assortment of goods belonging to the Hudson Bay Company. There are also a good store, kept by a Frenchman, post office, waggon shop and blacksmith shop, and several private residences. In the neighborhood is a saw and grist mill, owned by John Baptist, who is the possessor of 500 acres of arable land. This settlement, extending for miles down the Seine, is in the

DISTRICT OF PROVENCHER,

Louis Riel's constituency, known as St. Anne's. The inhabitants are principally French half-breeds. I noticed that a few days after I left the Province, Riel, that misguided individual, had been re-elected. It is very evident that Riel is popular with his people. But what possible excuse can he have for thrusting himself upon them for re-election after being expelled from the House as a fugitive from justice ? After enjoying a comfortable meal, and taking a stroll through the village, we made preparation for extending our trip. Oak Point is thirty miles from Fort Garry. On our route we cross one of the richest prairies in the Province. The ground is covered with lovely flowers and rich grass. Thousands of tons of hay may be cut yearly. Annual cutting would also improve the grass ; it would become much finer and sweeter. The road in places is soft, but you can deviate from the track on either side at pleasure. Some 12 miles bring us to a French settlement on a bend of the Seine. A few Irish settlers have located themselves in this neighborhood. One McQuade told us the difficulties he had to encounter with the half-breeds, who were very jealous of any other class of people settling amongst them ; how they had come at night, torn down his house, thrown down his fences, and that while he was thatching his house several came with guns loaded and threatened to shoot him unless he would leave. However, he persisted, put them at defiance, and is now in the occupation of a good farm, with several sons on adjoining farms. The poor man was leaning against the fence, lamenting the sad havoc and destruction the grasshoppers had made of his crop. Being somewhat isolated from other settlers, the grasshoppers had made a clean sweep of his crops, including even his roots.

A PRIMITIVE VEHICLE.

Proceeding a little further, we met an immigrant who had purchased at the office in Winnipeg a claim, and was on his way to inspect the premises. He was perched on a Red River cart, constructed entirely of wood, not a particle of iron whatever. They are in general use. Traders find them more serviceable than any other vehicle. You can hear the screeching of the wheels for a mile. They are scarcely ever greased. The cart was drawn by a single ox harnessed with strips of ox hide. Late at night we arrived at St. Boniface, the residence of Bishop Taché. adjoining which the Catholic cathedral towers above all others. The site is beautiful. On the east side of the Red river, at the confluence with the Assiniboine, the mission holds possession of several thousand acres of the best agricultural land in the Province. The lots adjoining the river sell rapidly for $1000 per acre. The Red river is a very important stream, wide, sufficiently deep, and is navigable for nearly seven hundred miles. Its waters are turbid, owing to the loose nature of the soil on its banks. Some of the oldest settlers assert that the river near Winnipeg is nearly double the width now that it was at the time they first entered the Province. Crossing the ferry on a peculiarly constructed flat bottom boat, fastened to a chain strung across the river, driven by the current and moving at considerable speed, we landed at Winnipeg, drove to the "Exchange hotel" and succeeded in getting comfortable quarters. Our first desire was to ascertain whether we had lost our capacity for eating and drinking. We had hitherto strictly adhered to teetotal principles—through absolute necessity, since our supply of Henessey had become contraband. Temperance principles prevail all along the Dawson Route. No intoxicating liquors are tolerated. Notwithstanding all the drawbacks, the

DAWSON ROUTE

affords one of the most enjoyable excursions on the continent of America—full of interest to the artist, botanist, mineralogist and geologist ; the whole route is so varied, the scenery so romantic and grand beyond description, no person can form the faintest conception of its grandeur and magnificence without a personal inspection. A sportsman can find an attractive field at both ends of the route, and on the portage prairie hens, ducks, pigeons, deer and moose are plentiful. For the angler those silvery lakes supply abundance of fish. The flies are certainly troublesome for a month or six weeks in the season, and if you are not furnished with a palatable bill of fare, put a curb upon your appetite and feed yourself with promises. Occasional fasting will do good. Your stomach will not be clogged with indigestible dainties, and after you return you can better appreciate the sweets of civilization and domestic life.

I promised at the outset to carry the reader with me to Fort Garry, in two letters, but it has taken four. Had I acted on my promise, I should have been under the necessity of jumping from pillar to post. I am in duty bound to give an unvarnished description of our ramblings, and the reader must exercise patience, provided he expects to travel in our company. In my next we will proceed through the various settled portions of the Province of Manitoba.

Yours truly,

JAMES TROW.

———

DEAR Sir,—After partaking of the bounties of life at the "Exchange hotel", we experienced quite a reaction ; our blood began to flow more freely, our cheeks resumed their natural color, and we rejoiced that we were born with the desire and capacity for enjoyment. No person can properly appreciate sweets unless they occasionally taste sour things. Retiring for the night, we had the satisfac- tion of divesting ourselves of garments that had not been removed for eleven nights in succession. Notwithstanding our discomforts, we were highly delighted with the trip.

THE DAWSON ROUTE—SUGGESTIONS.

With an outlay legitimately and judiciously expended of five or six millions of dollars, the Dawson Route could be made available for one of the most delightful excursions, which could be accomplished in less than half the time that is now required. A railway could easily be constructed from Winnipeg to the North West angle, a distance of 110 miles, or through our own territory, say 120 miles. There are no deep cuttings or engineering difficulties on the route, the entire line being either level or gently undulating, with sufficient drainage to keep the roadbed dry. The whole tract of country from the Angle to Oak Point is thickly covered with valuable timber, which will find a ready market for fence and building purposes. The supply at present is purchased in Minnesota and rafted down Red River to Winnipeg; millions of acres that now could not be given away would readily sell for $3 to $5 per acre, creating a revenue more than sufficient to construct the road. Bridging on the route would be very trifling. The only rivers are White Birch, White Mud, Broken Head Creek, and the Seine—all small rivers. A large expenditure would be necessary to construct a bridge across the Red River at Winnipeg, owing to the loose nature of the soil on the river banks. To travel that portion of the road by stage now occupies three days, but it could be accomplished by rail in as many hours. Thousands of immigrants would settle along the line of road. The land is not as well adapted for agricultural purposes as the rich prairie or river lands, the soil being much lighter; but similar lands are cultivated in many parts of Minnesota and in Northern Wisconsin. The landing at the Angle should be on British soil, and not as at present on the Minnesota side. Some dredging is required at the mouth of Rainy River and a light house constructed; the channel for miles properly buoyed through the shallow waters of the Lake of the Woods, the boulders blasted and removed out of the Sault and Manitou rapids, and a lock constructed at Fort

Francis. Then steamers could run without interruption from the Angle to Kettle Falls, about 200 miles, in a day, while under present arrangements this portion of the route often takes four days, never less than three. Many of the other lakes could be connected together, some of the various portages overcome by the construction of locks and dams so that bulk would not have to be broken so frequently, and a railway made from Shebandowan to Prince Arthur's Landing, 45 miles. Should these works be completed, passengers and their baggage could be comfortably carried from one end of the Dawson route to the other in five days less than the time it now takes with large steamers from Winnipeg to Moorhead up the Red River. This water route would be of great service to the Dominion, even after the Pacific Railway was constructed; and water communication is decidedly cheaper than rail. The works could all be accomplished in one season. The Pacific Railway may not be completed for many years to come. If we expect to induce immigrants to settle in the Great North West, we must have immediate facilities to convey them with speed through our own country.

THE CAPITAL OF THE PRAIRIE PROVINCE.

. Winnipeg is beautifully situated at the confluence of the Assiniboine with the Red River, on a plateau or level prairie. The river, during the infancy of the settlement, overflowed its banks and flooded the prairie for miles round. This was owing to the melting of the ice further south in Minnesota, and the course being north, the ice bound river through Manitoba dammed back the water. The consequence was the whole country side was frequently flooded, but of late years the spring thaws have been more regular and gradual, and the bed of the river is much wider. No danger apparently exists now. Part of the town is regularly laid out, and the streets lead into each other very conveniently. Other parts of the town are the reverse of this. This state of things is brought about by so many different surveys. Town lots realize fabulous prices, and every owner of a piece of land within a radius of a mile from the centre of the town subdivides his farm or homestead, and makes a distinct survey of his property. We noticed numerous substantial buildings, stores, private residences; and many commodious structures of white brick, manufactured in the neighborhood, are in course of construction. The Dominion Government are putting up two good brick buildings —the land office and Inland Revenue department, upon sites purchased from the Hudson Bay Co. A new post office is much needed, the present building being a miserable, dilapidated shanty on a back street, —totally unfitted for the business of the place. The streets are wide, and after a shower of rain exceedingly dirty. Mayor Cornish is alive to the necessities of the case and has this season more side walks under contract than were ever before made. The town has also been properly assessed for the first time, and all property holders will be compelled to contribute in proportion to their means towards the municipal government and public improvements. To many the visit of the tax collector will be both strange and unwelcome. The rate will be very high, the town having debts to meet and works under construction which are all to be wiped out with this year's taxes. Much better would it have been if the town council had issued debentures, payable in twenty years, for the construction of water works, sewerage, and other necessary public works. The tax would thus be light upon present property holders, and others who may become citizens and property holders hereafter would bear their share of the burden.

HIGH RENTS.

Rents at present are enormous. A dwelling-house containing five or six rooms will rent for $50 per month. A medium sized store or business place, in a central position, will realise $1,500 or $2,000 per annum. " Davis' hotel, " a frame building, cut up in the most inconvenient manner, and which would not fetch for the deed in fee simple in the city of Toronto, $6,000, rents for $5,000, and the store in one end of the building for $1,000 more. Hon. Mr. Davis, the proprietor, paid for the entire premises a few years ago, $10,000. Many vacant town lots on Main-street could not be purchased for $2,000. The Hudson Bay Co. are in possession of the most eligible portion of the town, and are disposing of lots at fabulous figures. Two years ago the company held an auction sale and disposed of 13 acres for $7,000 per acre. The Company claim 500 acres at Upper Fort Garry. The late Minister of the Interior, Hon. Mr. Aikins, informed me that 50 acres were retained by the Government, most likely that portion of the town on which the barracks are erected. Some legerdemain, or sleight of hand work, by the late Administration, transferred this valuable tract of land to the Company, for under the terms of agreement, it was understood that in the Red River Settlement the size of the block to be retained round Upper Fort Garry should not exceed 10 acres, and that round Lower Fort Garry was not to be in excess of 300 acres. The stipulations were, that the Dominion was to pay the Company £300,000, or one and a half million dollars in money, the Company to retain the posts they actually occupied in the North West Territory, and to select blocks adjoining their stations, within twelve months after the surrender, not to exceed in the aggregate 50,000 acres. The Co. may at any time within 50 years after the surrender claim in any township or district one-twentieth part of the land, and were allowed to make choice in any township for ten years after its survey, in accordance with this agreement, the Company made selections of 117 blocks varying in size from five acres to 3000 acres—the most valuable and eligible locations for town and villages in the North West, comparatively speaking the cream of the whole country ; and chose 45,160 acres (leaving 4,840 yet to be selected) having taken the precaution at that period to leave the portions selected at the Upper and Lower Fort Garry to a more convenient season. A saving clause was inserted in the terms of agreement that at

UPPER AND LOWER FORT GARRY

such number of acres should be reserved as might be agreed upon between the Company and the Governor of Canada in council. We all know what this means. The Pacific contract was let, and was to be constructed under similar regulations. Much better would it have been if the Dominion had agreed to pay the Company ten millions of dollars for their imaginary claim, than to allow that great monopoly such extraordinary privileges. Large landed monopolies are a curse to any country ; they never contribute a fair proportion of taxation. To crown all, the Government undertakes to compensate the legitimate owners (the Indians) for their claims to lands required for purposes of settlement, relieving the Company from all responsibility, and guaranteeing to the Company peaceable possession. This Company obtained its charter, from King Charles, in 1670 to a territory 2,600 miles long and 1,400 miles broad. Many eminent lawyers have given their opinion that the rights conferred were only for the trading purposes, and without any right to the soil. Just as soon as the country became settled the Company should surrender their rights. In 1783, the North West Company, composed of Canadians from Montreal, entered the North West, and disputed the claim of the Hudson Bay Company. The rival companies then armed their agents and servants, and many battles were fought, resulting ultimately in the amalgamation of the rival companies. The officers were not paid a fix salary, but participated in a share of the profits. In 1811 the Earl of Selkirk purchased from the Hudson Bay Company, a large tract of land on Red River and the Assiniboine, subject to the Indian claims. The Earl induced a great number of settlers from the country of Sutherland, Scotland, to immigrate to this distant colony, and for many years they endured great hardships and privations. The rival companies regarded them as intruders, and the poor settlers were continually harassed both by the servants of the other companies and by hostile Indians. Many were killed, and their little habitations destroyed. Ultimatly a pitched battle was fought at a place called Seven Oaks, a large number being killed, including Governor Semple. Some time afterwards, Lord Selkirk visited the settlement and purchased from the Indians two miles back on either side of the Red River from its mouth, extending to Red Lake River in the United States, and along the Assiniboine from its junction to Muskrat River. The only way to convey to the Indian mind a distance of two miles was by indicating the greatest distance at which a horse on the level prairie could be distinctly seen, or daylight seen under his belly.

Lord Selkirk died in 1821, and in 1836 the Hudson Bay Co. repurchased from his heirs the lands ceded to him in 1811. The Company

IMPOSED SOME VERY ARBITRARY RULES

upon the settlers. No person was allowed to purchase any furs from an Indian or sell any furs to any person other than the Company's agents, under the risk of a criminal prosecution. No person trading could send a private letter beyond the Province by the Company's packet, unless open for inspection by the Company's agents. If any furs were found in the possession of any farmer, the Company would punish him by refusing to purchase any of his produce. Since the surrender by the Company, the town of Winnipeg is growing as if by magic in every direction, but where nature desired the town should stand, is at the confluence of the two great rivers, and that portion is under the iron hand of that great monopoly. No town with which I am acquainted has grown more rapidly than Winnipeg. There come annually many permanent settlers ; and all who are possessed of sober, industrious habits, yearly increase in wealth. The town is possessed of many good business men, who are expending large sums to advance the interests of the place ; the extent of the population is matter of conjecture, a variety of opinions prevailing as to the number of its citizens. Judging from the area of the place and the amount of business places and private residences, I would consider that the town contained at least between five and six thousand inhabitants.

WINNIPEG IS THE HUB

of the North West. An immense trade is centred in this place. The town must rapidly increase in wealth and population. The resources of the country are great, if properly developed. The Province of Manitoba is the smallest in the Dominion, containing only 14,340 square miles, nearly 9,000,000 acres of land, while the North West contains 2,750,000 square miles. The bounds of the Province should be enlarged to at least double their present dimensions. The expenses of carrying on the Local Government would not be much increased, and intending settlers would have a larger field to select from. The greatest drawback to the rapid settlement of the Province, and to the prosperity of Winnipeg in particular, is that so much of the surrounding country is locked up from actual settlement. The land is divided into a strip on each side of the principal rivers, four miles in depth, making very inconvenient farms. Many are not more than from four to six chains in width, fronting the river, and some are even less, and have more the appearance of a street than a farm. This provision was first made for the purpose of having the settlers as close together as possible, for self-defense against the incursions of the " untutored savage." The remainder of the lands in the Province is surveyed into townships of six miles square, and subdivided into sections of one mile square, exclusive of road allowance. The roads are two chains in width. In the Western States townships are surveyed out in a similar manner, but no road allowance is left, and the settler, through a road superviser, makes provision for roads to suit the convenience of the people. The consequence is the roads are zig zag, and after the country becomes settled, very inconvenient. The

next great drawback is a reserve containing one million
and a half acres selected in the centre of the Province, set
apart for the offspring of the half breeds round the town of
Winnipeg. These lands were set apart for the minor children under a Dominion statute, to be distributed by lot.
Some 18 years must yet elapse before many of these minors are of age, and is it reasonable that the best portions
of the Province should be kept unsettled for such a time?
Much better would it be for the country if the lands were
set apart for all who have attained their majority, and
the balance sold and the funds invested by trustees.

ANOTHER RESERVATION,

which gives great dissatisfaction, is that one twentieth be-
longs to the Hudson Bay Company. One-eighteenth, it
appears, is set apart, being sections No. 8 and 26, 1280
acres, in each township ; eight or most probably 10 townships are reserved for the Menonnites. This is a good provision, for the lands will be immediately settled and under
cultivation. (I shall treat upon the Mennonites and their
reserve in future letters.) We also find four townships
reserved for the Emerson colony, a mere sham, or speculation. There are also an Indian reserve and 1280 acres
in each township reserved for educational purposes—a very
wise provision. The consequence of these reservations is
that the poor immigrant or actual settler who desires to
carve out for himself a home, is under the necessity of
locating far remote from market on the outskirts of the
Province, and would willingly submit, providing those numerous reservations were settled and under cultivation.
But to be under the necessity of travelling 20 or 30 miles
through an unsettled country to market or places of bu-

siness, the roads of necessity being unimproved and very bad in spring and fall, is very discouraging. The roads in summer are very good. The traveller is not confined to any particular limits, but can deviate from the track round soft or marshy places. The stage road from Winnipeg to Pembina, the road from Winnipeg past the Portage to the Province line, from Winnipeg to the Stone fort, also the road from Winnipeg to Oak Point, are kept up at the expense of the Province, but very little repairs are made on them, excepting a few bridges thrown across ravines or creeks. The roads are chiefly level, there being no grades or cuttings. There are no mountains or hills, the entire Province being one vast plain, varied only by gentle undulations. These elevations are rare, and form marked landmarks in the landscape. Occasionally we find what are called saddle backs, an elevation sloping off on each side, evidently the gatherings and washings of opposing currents.

THE SCENERY IS BEAUTIFUL,

.

but I thought if nature had scattered here and there promiscuously a few hills, the country would be much better and more sheltered from storms.

Having killed off the first day and a few old hours of the second, in visiting old acquaintances, such as our esteemed friend the Chief Justice, who is quite elated with the country, Dr. Schultz, M. P., who has given over his extensive practice and finds the fur trade more profitable, we dined with Mayor Cornish, who is driving a lucrative practice. We left in the afternoon for Prairie Portage, distant some seventy miles. My next letter will describe the grasshopper plague and our journeyings through the settled portion of the Province.

Yours truly,

JAMES TROW.

Dear Sir,—I stated in my last letter that the Hudson Bay Co. claimed within the corporation of the city of Winnipeg, 500 acres of great value. By referring to the Toronto *Globe* of the 16th inst. the reader will notice that on the 15th inst., the Company sold by auction between 25 and 30 acres of this reservation, subdivided into lots 50 by 100 feet, at from $600 to $700 per lot, and realizing a total of over $100,000, thus proving conclusively that the reservation at Winnipeg will net the Co. at least one and a half million of dollars, equivalent to the whole purchase in cash of £300,000 sterling for their imaginary claim to the whole North West territory. Many honest, industrious settlers claim the right of pre-emption to this reserve, and are preparing to test their right in a court of law. Much better would it have been for the Government of Sir John A. Macdonald to have encouraged the actual settler, than to transfer, for no equivalent whatever, such a valuable tract of land to this huge monopoly. If 500 acres can be sold for one and a half to two millions of dollars, can we estimate the enormous wealth they possess in the territory ? 50,000 acres—the most eligible locations—and also one-twentieth of the territory will be drained of its wealth for centuries to come, and the stockholders of this great monopoly and their offspring will live in luxury and splendor in the great cities of Britain on the hard earnings of the poor settlers of the North West.

To resume our meanderings. We left Winnipeg for Portage la Prairie, distant 70 miles west, by the course of the Assiniboine, along the travelled tract leading to the Saskatchewan valley, crossing a flat prairie of sandy loam, many portions under crop. The road and fences were

LITERALLY COVERED WITH GRASSHOPPERS.

Millions were seen winging their way to the eastward. In looking towards the sun the sight resembled a heavy snow storm of large flakes, passing through the air with great rapidity. They were upon the ground piled one upon another so that we crushed thousands with every revolution of the carriage wheels. For the novelty of the thing, we would occasionnally alight and walk ahead of the horses, when millions would rise out of our path. On close examination thousands appeared stuck to the earth in a perpendicular position, their extremities indented in the earth nearly half the length of the body, in the act of depositing their eggs. We carefully examined these deposits, and found thousands of eggs deposited in a square foot, where the soil happened to be soft loam and free from grass. By scraping off the soil, an inch in depth, we could see the ground perforated with holes as if made with the end of a pointed stick. Many of these holes were empty, some were full, and others partially so. The eggs were closely packed together, placed in a perpendicular position, uniform in size, about the eighth of an inch in length and fully the thickness of a knitting needle. I examined many, and found from 50 to 70 eggs in a nest, carefully enveloped in a transparent covering. It is remarkable that these eggs are not destroyed in a country where the frost pene-

trates to such a depth, and where it is of such long conti-
nuance.

GRASSHOPPERS—THEORIES CONCERNING THEM.

Some allege that the eggs have been deposited so early in
the season that the excessive heat of summer incubates
them in the fall; others profess to have discovered a parasite under the wing of the female, and assert that when the
eggs are deposited, the parasite drops in the nest and des-
troys the germs. I sincerely hope the latter of these the-
ories will prove to be correct, so that the poor settlers may
be relieved from this plague. The crops were unusually
good this season. The farming community were greatly
elated at their favorable prospect; but in a few days their
hopes were blighted, their calculations falsified, and many
who were in comfortable circumstances got discouraged and
sold out their little homesteads to speculators and new
comers, at a great sacrifice. I can scarcely describe the
depressing effects produced by the ravages of the grasshoppers. Scores of intending settlers who had made their
calculations to remain in the Province, emulating Job's
comforters, took special interest in showing to immigrants
the dark side of the picture, and impressing on them that
next season the grasshoppers would sweep all before them,
that total starvation would inevitably prevail, that provisions would be enormously high the ensuing winter, owing
to the excessive freight for goods by land from Moorehead,
and that hundreds would depend on charity for sustenance
during the winter! Such lachrymose persons are to be
found in all communities—people who take a special interest
in exaggerating and fomenting troubles. Instead of stating
facts, that only one-third of the wheat crop had been des-

troyed; that there was sufficient raised in the Province un-
injured to maintain a much larger population; that peas
were excellent, and that root crops were abundant; that
land was cheap and fertile ; that the Dominion Government
were about to carry on extensive public works, and that all
who felt disposed to work could readily get employment;
the "comforters" I have mentioned took special delight in
picturing the dark side of the question. Grasshoppers are
to be found occasionally in all countries. In Ontario our
crops are frequently partially destroyed by weevil, midge,
and even grasshoppers, particularly where the soil is light
and warm. During the early settlement of the Western
States everything they raised was swept away periodically
for years. I am persuaded that when those extensive fertile prairies are broken up, the soil turned over, pulverized
and exposed to the winter frosts and a larger surface put
under cultivation, the damage done will scarcely be noticed.
I found in my travels through the Province, that where the
grasshoppers found an isolated settler they took all he had,
but in older and more extensive settlements the wheat crop
was but little injured, and should the grasshoppers destroy
one-half the wheat crop, the remaining half will yield
nearly as much per acre as the whole crop in any of the
other Provinces. Barley and oats have not been raised
very extensively in Manitoba, and when we hear that all
has been destroyed, it don't amount to much, for two-thirds
of the farmers had not a bushel of either barley or oats
sown.

ADVENT OF THE PLAGUE.

Grasshoppers first made their appearance in Manitoba in
1818, doing some damage ; the following year they destroyed the entire crop. The Province was then relieved

from their ravages till the year 1857, a period of 38 years. In 1858 a young brood hatched from the deposits of the previous year, swept over the Province in clouds but did no perceptible damage. In 1864 and in 1868 their ravages were more seriously felt. Their stay may now be terminated till next season and probably they will not do any damage for another quarter of a century. All kinds of experiments have been tried in other countries to do away the grasshopper plague.

Proceeding on our way we pass, near silver Heights, an extensive brewery with all the contrivances for doing a large business, but owing either to the scarcity of barley, the want of taste on the part of the half-breeds for beer, preferring fire water, or an Order in Council of the Dominion Government, prohibiting the manufacturing of beer outside the city of Winnipeg, the proprietors stopped manufacturing the beverage. I understand the brewery was recently sold for less than one half of the original cost. At

SILVER HEIGHTS,

we pass the splendid residence of the Hon. James McKay, a wealthy half-breed. His dwelling and outhouses are decorated with emblems of the chase, considerable taste being displayed about the premises. A few weeks afterwards I paid a second visit to Mr. McKay's and found his gardens totally destroyed by the grasshoppers. Numbers of Indians and half-breeds were lounging about the premises making preparations for a trip to the Rocky Mountains or Saskatchewan. Carts drawn by oxen and Indian ponies were hitched up ready for the start, the average load weighing from 800 to 1,000 lbs. They travel from 25 to

30 miles a day. Horses are used for lighter loads, such as tents and personal baggage. I noticed several carts loaded with dried buffalo, and pemmican. The latter is usually put up in bags, weighing 100 lbs., two feet long, one and a half feet wide and six inches thick. Like the Milesian's stew, it is "good, cooked and uncooked, boiled or stewed," and is almost exclusively used by Indians, half-breeds or traders. The Indian mode of preparation is to cut strips of buffalo meat and dry thoroughly in the sun, then pound with a club as fine as possible, put layer after layer in small bags, made of buffalo skins, and on every layer pour hot fat of the buffalo, which saturates the whole mass. When properly made, it will keep for 40 or 50 years. A pound of this preparation with bread will be sufficient for a large family for a meal. The Hon. Jas. McKay is reputed to be very wealthy, and is a great trader. Himself and his amiable partner appear to thrive, for their united weight exceeds 500 lbs. A short distance further we pass the late residence of Mr. Donald A. Smith, M. P., chief manager of the Hudson Bay interest in the North West. For a few miles further the country is settled by half-breeds, who make very indifferent farmers and who devote most of their time to trading for Mr. McKay, Dr. Schultz, or the Hudson Bay Company. We soon enter and cross

A BEAUTIFUL ROLLING PRAIRIE

for many miles round, almost as far as the eye extends, totally bare of trees, and the horizon unbroken excepting in the direction of the Assiniboine. Proceeding onwards we cross Sturgeon Creek, a beautiful settlement, many of the farms well fenced and under tolerable cultivation. We were introduced to one John Grant, a half-breed, who owns probably 2,000 acres of land in the Province, keeps numerous herds of oxen and ponies, and hires them out for the season. Mr. Grant informed me that he had upwards of 100 horses, which he invariably turned out in winter to shift for themselves, and that he generally found them in spring in excellent condition. Mr. Grant also owns a large stock-farm in the Boyne settlement, distant some 40 miles from his residence on Sturgeon Creek. A short drive brought us to Headingly, where the notorious Lord Gordon committed suicide. Gordon's melancholy death created great excitement in Winnipeg. The New York officials who attempted to kidnap him had their business well planned, but they were sadly foiled. About sunset we arrived at the station kept by Mr. House, an American, and put up for the night. Shortly afterwards Lieutenant-Governor Morris and Mrs. Morris, with some of the juvenile members of the family, drove up and stayed all night. We found Governor Morris and his amiable lady very sociable and agreeable. We travelled in their company the following day to Portage la Prairie and through the settlements, whither the Governor was *en route* in order to ascertain from personal observation the

DAMAGES DONE BY THE GRASSHOPPERS.

Governor Morris is a thin spare man of medium height, having a striking resemblance to Sir John Macdonald, but much younger. After the rest had retired, I was entertained by the landlord with a rehearsal of his imprisonment

by Riel, how he frequently disobeyed the pseudo " Presi-'
dent's " orders, put him at defiance, and threatened ven-
geance if he dared to imprison an American citizen; how
he had marched with the Portage men past the Fort to
Kildonan, expecting to unite their forces, &c., &c. He
stated that 100 resolute men could have taken both Riel
and his forces without much blood-s'ed.

Travelling in company with the Governor and family
next morning, we followed the beaten track round the east
side of the Bay of St. Paul's. The Governor considered it
much safer than risking a nearer drive across the centre of
the Bay, which is evidently the bottom of a large lake,
either raised by vegetable growth or some other cause.
Thousands of tons of hay are annually cut in this marsh.
Mr. House the previous year had let a contract for cutting
and stacking 100 tons for $1.50 per ton. We dined at
Poplar Point and partook sumptuously of prairie chickens,
very acceptable fare after our morning's exercise over the
broad prairies. The soil in this locality is rich and very
productive. I took a stroll with the landlord over his fields,
examined his crops, to which the grasshoppers had certainly
done great injury, but he felt thankful, saying "half a crop
is much better here than what we considered a good crop
in Lanark, Ontario." We noticed many beau 'f ' poplar
groves, and on the opposite side of the Assinib he, trees
of considerable size were seen extending for miles up the
river. Near to Poplar point we passed

AN INDIAN ENCAMPMENT

containing some thirty or forty families of the Sioux tribe.
This tribe invariably camps on the open prairie, far removed from the bush, It is stated that they are in dread of

the Chippewas, who fight better under cover, and that the
Sioux are a match for them on the open plain. Many hundreds of this tribe crossed the border from Minnesota after
the massacre in 1862. The men are straight and tall, and
apparently very lazy. Several have no covering but a
blanket and breech cloth, their hair jet black, hanging down
their backs. Many have their faces painted with a variety
of colors; some red, with blue stripes; others blue and
yellow stripes; others have long feathers stuck in their
hair, while some have to be content with only one feather.
(It is alleged that each feather denotes the number of
scalps in their possession.) When driven across the border
a large number of them had neither guns nor ammunition;
and their very existence depending upon the chase, they
were reduced to actual starvation. Their chiefs and lead-
ers made repeated applications to the Government for provisions or fire arms, so that they might support themselves.
The Government could not agree to furnish them with arms
and ammunition so long as they were at war with the United
States; and the Province not having any surplus provisions, hundreds of them died during the winter. The main
cause of the outbreak was want of faith kept with the Indians by American agents. A certain pension or allowance
was granted them per annum. They had years before the
outbreak ceded over to the United States Government,
large tracts of lands. The poor Indians and their families
were called together at certain periods to receive their small
pittance; the agents would keep them waiting for weeks
and in some cases months, all the provisions they brought
with them being in the interval exhausted; and being far
remote from their hunting grounds they were often in a
famishing condition. They frequently made an appeal for
money due them, or food; and in the absence of either,

scores died from actual starvation. This state of things was repeated again and again, culminating in

A GENERAL MASSACRE.

The Indians were determined to slaughter every man, woman or child occupying the lands they had ceded. The consequence was, through the conduct of a few overbearing, grasping officials, 1,600 defenceless settlers were butchered in cold blood. The Sioux Indians appear more indolent than the Chippewas; they lounge about their camps depending almost entirely upon what the squaws can beg from the settlers, or upon the sale of berries or baskets, &c. The more they get for their labor the less they will do; and the more an article brings them the less they will fetch to market. Their wants are few and easily satisfied. I noticed their mode of roasting fish with some interest. The fish is fixed on the end of a stick, two feet long, one end in the ground at the side of the fire, the other end leaning over the fire; the roasting is generally well done, but the process is slow. There is no excuse, particularly in the summer season, for Indians to be begging. On Long Lake hundreds of wild ducks were seen, and prairie chickens are so plentiful that. they could frequently be struck with a club. Manitoba Lake, only distant 10 miles, is stocked with excellent fish. While roaming over the prairies a few hundred miles west are large herds of buffaloes which are easily captured. The climate is such that buffalo meat can easily be dried and kept for years. The buffaloes have been driven far west and are yearly recklessly slaughtered by tens of thousands, merely for their hides and tongues, the carcase wasted, while hundreds of Indians are suffering partial starvation every winter, many of them dying from absolute want. Some measures of protection should at once be enacted, or the alternative will be the buffalo will soon become extinct.

Proceeding 11 or 12 miles across an undulating prairie, covered with rich luxuriant grass and

A PROFUSION OF LOVELY FLOWERS,

on which are no sandy or gravel ridges, no swamps or marshes, and every foot capable of producing abundant crops, we arrived at High Bluffs, and were kindly entertained by Mrs. Allcock and family, formerly of Mitchell, and Mr. Wm. Moss, late of Mornington. These parties left Ontario with considerable means, which they invested largely in real estate, and they are now the owners of extensive farms, upwards of 1,000 acres each, with comfortable buildings and apparently surrounded with all the elements of comfort and civilization, such as schools, churches, postal privileges, &c. Their crops were excellent, but partially destroyed by the grasshoppers. Quite a settlement of Canadians who left the county of Perth are located in this neighborhood—Mr. Whimster, of Blanchard, Mr. Small, of Logan, and Mr. Jerrald, teacher. All are doing remarkably well and are in comfortable circumstances. Early in the morning we continued our journey westward. For the first two or three miles we travel through a good settlement. On the rest of the road to the Portage we found here and there a settler commencing life on the open prairie. Far away in the distance, along the outskirts of the wood, the landscape is studded with comfortable homesteads. Between the English settlement and the Portage we cross a rolling prairie, rising gradually till we arrive at the village, near which, on the open plain, a tribe of Saulteaux or Bungees were encamped, probably numbering 50 or 60 families. Their tents had a much cleaner and more respectable appearance than those of the Sioux, yet on close inspection we found the inmates slovenly and extremely filthy in their habits. Could not those able-bodied natives and their families be taught habits of industry and become cultivators of the soil? Five acres under crop—wh t. potatoes and vegetables—would contribute more towards their comfort than all they earn by the chase.

PORTAGE LA PRAIRIE,

or prairie portage, was named by Indians or traders, who had of necessity to carry their canoes across this prairie from the Assiniboine to Lake Manitoba, distant some 12 miles. The village is beautifully situated on the table land, somewhat elevated above the surrounding prairies. The village proper contains a tavern, two stores, blacksmith and waggon shops. In this neighborhood we met one Mr. McLean, a Highlander, an old settler, who is the possessor of a splendid farm, and has in course of construction the best farm house in the settlement. McLean had been reading the local press of Manitoba about the dreadful ravages of the grasshoppers, and said it was a shame to make such a howl, that there was more grain left in the Province than all the inhabitants could consume for two years

In my next we will pay a visit to Mr. Kenneth McKenzie and Mr. Hugh Grant, two of the largest and most successful agriculturists in Manitoba, and will also allude to other settlements within the Province.

Yours truly,

JAMES TROW.

DEAR SIR,—In my last communication we parted with the reader at Portage la Prairie, and were about proceeding to Rat Creek. But prior to leaving, we must, as a matter of interest, interview Mr. John McLean, the oldest pioneer in the locality. Mr. McLean emigrated from the neighborhood of Guelph, Province of Ontario, some years ago, and is quite a character. He wished to ascertain, as a preliminary, if we were sincere in our intentions of becoming permanent settlers. If so, he recommended us to purchase a moderately sized farm not to exceed a quarter of a section (160 acres), saying that he was content with that quantity, and probably realized as much profit from his estate as many who roamed over many sections. His policy was distribution, and not centralization. The country, he thought, should be subdivided into innumerable homesteads, and distributed to *bona fide* settlers. Very many, he said, came to Manitoba with extravagant notions and great expectations, who were accustomed to a life of idleness, luxury and ease. The charms of novelty, change of situation and the expectations of amassing a fortune (without labor), had induced them to immigrate. He could see daily many of these "feather-bed farmers" with dog and gun roaming over the prairies, and after a freshet, he had actually seen several of such "farmers," fishing over the ravines, or along the borders of the lake fronting his premises, on horseback. "What we really require," said Mr. McLean, with emphasis, "is men able and willing to till the soil; the natives can do all the fishing and hunting requisite." Mr. McLean condemned the

POLICY OF THE LATE ADMINISTRATION,

in regard to their mode of building the Pacific Railway; but strongly advocated the construction of a canal from the

Assiniboine through *his farm* to connect with Lake Manitoba. Before leaving the village we had an introduction to Mr. Joseph Ryan, M. P., now declared member for Marquette. Mr. Ryan was defeated by the late Mr. Cunningham, by 42 votes. A protest was entered and a scrutiny resulted in favor of Mr. Ryan. Evidently the Catholics of Manitoba are not the bigots some represent them to be; for we find in this division nearly all the Catholic vote polled for Cunningham, a Protestant, and nearly all the Protestants voting for Ryan, a Catholic. Mr. Ryan is a solicitor, resides at the Portage, and is an active, energetic man, enjoying a lucrative practice.

Crossing a lovely prairie of unbounded fertility we noticed many patches cultivated, the soil of which is a dark, rich loam ; the whole prairie extending as far as the eye could reach, free from any accumulation of green scum, ponds or stagnant water, which are so frequently met with in Minnesota and many of the Western States. The effluvia arising from these low places poisons the atmosphere, and fevers and death frequently result. The prairies of Manitoba are undulating. Occasionally these natural undulations swell into eminences of moderate height, creating natural drainage. This combined with the porous and friable nature of the soil, keeps the surface free from any accumulations of water. For miles round, nothing can be seen to impede the progress of the plough, no rocks, stones or stumps, but the broad prairie covered with a

PROFUSION OF SWEET SCENTED FLOWERS,

comprising numerous varieties of the rose, sun flower, wild pea and numberless others of every imaginable tint and color. This country is beautifully adapted for the raising of stock with very little expense or trouble. The great influx of immigration will create a ready and profitable market for years to come. Rat creek is an insignificant stream taking its rise some 10 or 12 miles south west from McKenzie's farm, and running north, empties into Lake Manitoba near Totogan, a town in prospective—better known upon paper than in the locality where it is supposed to exist. A temporary dam is thrown across this dirty creek at the rear of McKenzie's dwelling to gather water for family use. A geological party in the employ of the Dominion Government are at work near the yard boring for water, and had reached a depth of 150 feet without success. The engineer, a Mr. McDonald, showed our party the diamond drill which cost $5,000. It cuts a clean hole $1\frac{1}{2}$ inches in diameter out of the rock and brings up the innercore entire. I met with another party under Mr. Ward, bound for Fort Ellice, for the purpose of testing the land in that locality. Mr. Ward had procured the services of the half-breed, Grant, at an expense of $736, to take the machinery back. These test wells will be of great service to the settlers if successful.

We were very much disappointed to find that Mr. McKenzie had left home the previous day on a fishing excursion to Lake Manitoba. We fully expected to have gleaned valuable information from one so thoroughly posted in agriculture. However, his amiable partner kindly entertained our party, and gave us a general insight into the working of the farm. We carefully examined the crops; the oats and barley were almost totally destroyed by grasshoppers, the wheat crop, which was very large and good, was but partially injured. I noticed one field containing about 50 acres, north of the Saskatchewan road, the lower leaves of which had been stripped from the stalk, the straw being stiff and all erect; the heads erect and well filled; the probable yield would be from 27 to 30 bushels per acre. The potato and turnip crops were large and had a healthy appearance. Mr. McKenzie claims about 2000 acres on the home farm, 200 of which are improved and under crop. He also owns some 400 acres of bush land, and 320 acres of meadow.

CROSSING RAT CREEK,

we noticed encamped on the prairie, a large body of half-breeds, with probably 200 ox carts, preparing for a start to the Rocky Mountains, freighted with provisions and goods for the Indian trade. Mounting an enormous straw stack of the previous year's crop (as fresh as the day it was threshed, the pureness of the atmosphere preventing decomposition) we took special interest in witnessing the cavalcade moving westward. Scanning the horizon we observed a large herd of cattle in the distance, and concluded they were McKenzie's stock. Those of our company who felt disposed, crossed the prairie and examined this valuable herd. I counted 115 head of cattle, many thorough-bred, all in excellent condition, roaming at large over the broad prairie. The winters cannot be very severe, for I noticed that the only protection McKenzie has for his stock are miserable open sheds made of poles and covered with straw. We met Mr. Hugh Grant, formerly a resident of Brucefield county of Huron, who is in occupation of upwards of 1000 acres adjoining that of McKenzie, having 80 or 100 acres under cultivation. Mr. Grant states that the reported fabulous yield of grain per acre is not correct, that he is in a position to know, being in possession of a threshing machine and travels round in winter threshing. He had threshed last winter from 14,000 to 20,000 bushels of wheat, and he

would place the average crop of wheat at 30 bushels, oats
50, barley 40. Root crops were always good, and surpas-
sed in size and quality anything he ever saw. Mr. Grant
said he had resided three successive winters in the Province,
and experienced no discomfort from the cold, that the usual
depth of snow was a foot, quite light and scarcely ever
drifted; the winter sets in generally about the 9th or 10th
of November; that he was ploughing last fall the 25th of
October. He also stated that he had cattle out all winter,
that horses roam about uncared for the winter through, and
were found in splendid condition in spring. Great credit
is due to Messrs. McKenzie and Grant for

INTRODUCING IMPROVED BREEDS

of stock into the country and contributing so largely towards the annual exhibitions held at the portage. My firm
impression is that few countries are more desirable or inviting to the agriculturist, the mechanic or laboring man,
than the Province of Manitoba. The only drawback seems
to be the want of running streams, but I noticed many excellent wells of pure water only a few feet in depth. I have
observed that in all new settled countries the settlers will
carry water, let it be ever so bad, for some time for family
use before they put on resolution enough to dig a good well
at their door.

Returning from Rat River I used what I considered
plausible arguments to induce our company to diverge from
the Saskatchewan track homeward and come round by Totogan, south of Lake Manitoba through Woodland and Victoria settlements to Winnipeg, but my arguments were un-
availing, the Mayor concluding that he for one had seen
enough to satisfy any unprejudiced mind that the country

was only calculated for the Indian and buffalo or fur producing animals, and not for civilized society, that he would
not swap the town of Mitchell for the North West Territory. I made allowance for the Mayor's rash estimate of
the country, owing to his being a bachelor, and having
amassed a fortune in Mitchell, where he will leave a permanent monument to his enterprise and public spirit. Returning towards High Bluff, we overtook an Indian on foot who
had fanciful notions of his agility and swiftness. Making
an attempt to pass us, Mr. Alcock succeeded in urging our
teamster to the chase ; the Indian gave a yell and bounded
forward with extraordinary speed. I stretched myself back
in the seat and left the balance to Providence and our pos-
tilion. However we succeeded in winning the race, and
this was the first opportunity during four days that we had
of knowing that our horses could travel. Proceeding to
Long Lake we fell in with Mr. Ralston and colony, consist-
ing of some four or five families. A large number had left
him at Winnipeg and returned. Mr. Ralston informed me
that he had obtained from the Government four townships
outside the Province boundary, and also extensive timber
limits, and that he intended to lay out a village and erect
mills immediately. My opinion is that settlers will require
greater inducements to settle than Mr. Ralston is prepared
to offer, and that the proposed colony is more a matter of
the imagination than a reality. We will save the reader
the annoyance of travelling back to Winnipeg in our company. Suffice it to say that we reached the capital in safe-
ty, after a very pleasant drive. Returned to town, we
noticed the place illuminated in honor of the arrival of

FIVE HUNDRED MENNONITES,

who had spread broadcast among the leading merchants

and mechanics some $15,000 in gold for stock, provisions, and agricultural implements. One successful merchant sold 50 or 60 waggons at $100 each, which he had purchased at from $72 to $75, delivered, quite unsuitable in my opinion for the wants of emigrants. Much better would it have been for them had they bought as many Red River carts for $15 a piece. Many purchased yokes of oxen, and others spans of horses, for which they paid in many instances extravagant prices. Imported horses from Canada or any of the States do not thrive for the first season; they require a good deal of care and attention in winter and very many die owing to the change of climate, &c. These Mennonites have a reservation of eight townships, partly on Rat River, between Oak Point and Emerson Colony, near the south east corner of the Province. On four of the townships not a particle of wood is to be found; on the rest are found along the creeks and rivers, building timber and poplar groves. Those who inhabit the timber limits are to furnish those who have not, and those in occupation of meadow lands are to allow those who have no hay for their stock for a time to have all things in common. Those in possession of means will immediately erect buildings on their homesteads, and those who are not so fortunate will remain over winter in buildings erected by Mr. Jacob Y. Shantz, of Waterloo, who put up this season four buildings 100 feet by 16 each, subdivided into five apartments each, for which he received two or three sections of land. The buildings are to remain for five years, afterwards to become the property of Mr. Shantz. Some allege that the Mennonites are descendants of the Waldenses. Be this as it may, we know that they derive their name from Menno Simon, a native of Witmassam, born in Friesland, A. D. 1495. From the year 1537, for nearly three centuries, the

MENNONITES WERE A PERSECUTED PEOPLE,

and fled from one country to another. Many went to Russia, Prussia, and other parts of Europe, many settled with William Penn in Pennsylvania. We have in the county of Waterloo, Ontario, numerous families, descendents of those who emigrated to Canada from Pennsylvania 60 years ago. I have had dealings with this class of people amounting to many thousands of dollars, and never found but one that I would not take his word for any reasonable amount as readily as his note. Those who have now arrived from Russia I hope are only the nucleus of an extensive settlement, for they are certainly peaceable, industrious, honest settlers, who will in a few years, through economy and industry, make these luxuriant prairies blossom as the rose. These Mennonites, notwithstanding the trials, fatigues and hardships they had undergone in travelling from Russia, were ruddy with health, cheerful and contented. Mr. Shantz is deserving of great praise for his philanthropic efforts on behalf of these settlers. Mr. Hespeler, immigration agent at Winnipeg, who first interviewed these people in Russia, is certainly the right man in the right place. I have known him to leave Winnipeg with his conveyance, drive to the Mennonite settlement, some 50 or 60 miles, camp out, and remain for days and nights locating them and endeavoring to make them comfortable. Taking a tour through the immigrant sheds, some 32 apartments, with the agent, Mr. Hespeler, we noticed quite a contrast—many English and Irish families who had occupied the sheds for weeks while their husbands were working out, to save payment of rent, were continually grumbling, and had all imaginary complaints to make, while the poor Mennonites were necessitated to camp out, and were cheerful, happy and contented.

THE GERMAN MENNONITES

left Prussia and settled in Russia on account of religious
opinions held by them against military service. The Czar
of Russia promised them that they should be exempt and
also be allowed to educate their children in their own way,
but the present Czar refuses them these privileges. Mr.
Hespeler was commissioned by the Dominion Government
in 1872 to visit Berdiansk, South Russia, for the purpose
of inducing the Mennonites to emigrate to Manitoba. De-
legates from their body were sent out and visited Manitoba
in 1873, accompanied by J. Y. Shantz, and a contract was
entered into with our Government that they should receive
free grants of land, religious schools of their own, be exempt
from military service, have the privilege of affirming instead
of making oaths in courts of law, and certain other privileges
in regard to passage out. These settlers are peculiarly
adopted for settling in Manitoba; they are accustomed to
much inferior soil, cold winters, and they will find much
more timber in Manitoba than in settlements bordering on
the sea of Azov, Russia.

Sunday morning Mr. McVicar drove myself and the
Mayor to hear the Rev. Mr. Black, at Kildonan. Before
service commenced we took a stroll through the graveyard
and read the epitaphs of the dead, many of great age. I
see no better evidence of a healthy and thriving population
than in the absence of graves in the churchyard. I noticed
one remarkable instance of the anxiety of our Highland
friends to pay respect to the dead (or may be living). One
tombstone was erected to the memory of one Sutherland
who had left his home on a certain day and had never returned, his relatives taking it for granted that he was dead.

We will in our next carry the reader with us—to the Penitentiary!

Yours truly,

JAMES TROW.

DEAR SIR,—Proceeding through Winnipeg, *en route* for Stony Mountain, the site of the penitentiary now in course of construction, our curiosity was excited by noticing an unusual gathering of Indians lounging in front of the Crown Lands office. Generally speaking the natives locate themselves along rivers and streams remote from settlements, where game, fish, and fuel are plentiful. Upon enquiry we ascertained that the Minister of the Interior, Hon. Mr. Laird, had arrived in the Province and was the guest of Governor Morris, and that this motley crowd was a deputation of Sioux, waiting for an interview. Most probably they had put on their Sunday suits for the occasion, as several had no covering except an old dirty blanket short leggings, and breech cloth. Some were fantastically decorated with gewgaws. One old chief covered his nakedness with the remnant of an old scarlet cloak, with buttons on of home manufacture, about the size and shape of a horse shoe. His matted, black unkempt hair, was decorated with huge feathers. The old fellow strutted round quite majestically. Soon Mr. Laird, in company with Governor Morris and several other gentlemen, made his appearance. The Minister was easily recognized by the natives, for like Saul among the Prophets, he was head and shoulders above all the rest. The Indian custom is to look with adoration upon the tallest man of the tribe, and without any introduction,

the natives made for the Minister, who very good humoredly
gave each a hearty shake of the hand and proceeded to business. He had for interpreter, a good-looking lady, rather
embonpoint, a half-breed, who spoke English very fluently.
For nearly two weeks, Mr. Laird listened to all kinds of
complaints, some imaginary, no doubt, many who had for-
feited their rights to their homesteads by being absent over
six months, and the lands resold, and several complaints
from parties who had settled upon the Government reservation at Stony Mountain. However, the Minister exercised
great patience and became exceedingly popular during his
short stay.

MAKING A TREATY.

The great object of Mr. Laird's mission to the Province,
was to effect a treaty with the Crees, Salteaux, and other
tribes of Indians, regarding an extensive territory at Qu'
Appelle. This treaty was amicably arranged some weeks
afterwards in the following manner : each chief to receive
an annual subsidy of $25 ; each headman, not to exceed
four in a band, $15 ; and to every other Indian and every
member of the family, including his squaw, $5 ; every chief
and headman a new suit of clothes once in three years ; a
supply of ammunition to each tribe, not to exceed $750 in
value. The most encouraging clause is that those engaged
in agricultural pursuits are to receive implements of husbandry and seed grain ; and to each chief, one bull, four
cows and a chest of tools. To distribute the milk of human
kindness among these untutored savages, to gain their con-
fidence and good will, is certainly much better policy than
that which the Americans adopt—cheating them out of
their promised pittance, and advocating their extermination,

resulting in broils and atrocities upon hundreds and thousands of poor innocent settlers, such as occurred in that horrible massacre in Minnesota in 1862. Much better still, if practicable, that these Indians were taught habits of industry, and thrown upon their own resources, than dragging out a miserable existence, depending upon this pittance doled out yearly, which in very many cases does harm, being lavishly squandered in gambling and dissipation, and often finding its way into the pockets of the unscrupulous traders. Sam Slick relates an anecdote of a Russian officer, who had lost both arms. His comrades being under the necessity of feeding him daily, ultimately concluded to make him shift for himself or die. The result was he could soon use the knife and fork with his feet and was afterwards independent of his comrades.

THE BENEFITS OF MR. LAIRD'S MISSION.

Mr. Laird's sojournings among these wild scenes of nature, and travels among the boundless and fertile prairies, the future happy homes of many millions of the surplus population of the old world, will be productive of much good. In less than a quarter of a century, we will find the immigrants congregated from all parts of the globe to these fertile plains, surrounded with all the luxuries and refinements of civilized life. During his limited stay in Manitoba, he will see the propriety and absolute necessity of advising the immediate construction of railroads or some other means of communication with the older Provinces and outside world. He will learn what policy is best suited to induce immigrants to cast their lot in that remote Province, the utility of putting an immediate check upon reckless speculation by non-residents in real estate, and of giving no encouragement to large landed monopolies, who dry up the resources of any country and put a check on the legitimate cultivation of the soil. He will return to Ottawa, invigorated in health, having his well-balanced mind stored with pleasing recollections of his excursion to the Prairie Province.

Proceeding over a beaten track some 12 or 15 miles across an open prairie, we arrived at

STONY MOUNTAIN.

The reader will naturally imagine that we have great obstacles to surmount, and laborious climbing in order to ascend the mount, but the slope is gradual, nearly a mile from the base before you reach the summit, which is elevated by some extraordinary freak of nature fifty feet above the level of the surrounding country. Small eminences are here called mountains, as nature has deprived the inhabitants of Manitoba of romantic landscape, there being no upheavals or depressions, but a great surface of undulating prairies, with occasional knolls on which timber has obtained a foothold. Stony Mountain is one of those ornaments of nature's museum, representing her works for tens of thousands of years before man made his appearance on this planet. This landmark evidently shows the former level of the surrounding country, but by what agency this great work was accomplished, we are at a loss to determine. The view from the site of the penitentiary is exceedingly grand, an ocean of vast prairie being presented as far as the eye can reach, interspersed with undulations, small groups of trees and natural groves. To the north, distant some six or eight miles we see Victoria settlement with little log houses dotted here and there over the prairie. To the south, distant some fifteen miles across an unbroken prairie, can be seen plainly the city of Winnipeg and Kildonan settlement, with the majestic Red river flowing with its numerous meanderings northwards into Lake Winnipeg. Between these distant points, hundreds of cattle are quietly grazing among the tall grass. Scores of farmers are seen with their families, making hay miles from the settlements; and numerous ox carts crossing, loaded with hay in many directions, towards the settlements. Having quenched our thirst from a sparkling spring gushing from the rock, near a limekiln, where an inexhaustible quantity of limestone crops out, we drove to the temporary boarding houses put up by the contractors, and were introduced to Mr. Lecourt, the Government architect, who kindly showed us the plans of the penitentiary, more particularly that portion thereof now under contract. The building now in course of construction is only one-eight part of the contemplated structure. The contractors are Messrs. Barclay & Morrison, of Guelph, thoroughgoing practical business men. The sight is most romantic. The rock crops out in regular layers. The upper layer seems the best; lower down the stone appears honeycombed and rotten. Mr. Lecourt's opinion is that the terms of the contract should be changed, that stone would be more durable than brick, and the material excavated from the foundation would do a large portion of the work. The contractors had several men digging and puddling clay for brickmaking on the flats and calculated to make half a million this fall, close to the site of the building. Mr. Barclay pointed out to our party a large oval hole, probably 10 or 15 feet in diameter, scooped out of the rock, called the snake hole. Numerous skeletons were strewn around. This hole appears to be a great rendez-vous for the reptile tribe, for I noticed in a recent Manitoba paper that Mr. Barclay stated to the Hon. Mr. Laird that his workmen had killed and burned since they commenced the work, seven cart loads.

THE FUTURE OF THE COUNTRY.

Returning to the city in the cool of the evening, leisurely across that treeless prairie, the thought struck me how long will it be before that naked plain will be dotted with mansions, farm houses and pleasure groves ! Those in possession of prairie farms must of necessity plant trees, which if protected from cattle and annual fires, will in a few years grow large enough for fuel and fence timber, and will add very materially to the health of the inhabitants, attracting moisture and rain, embellishing the landscape and giving shelter to man and beast from storms which are always prevalent in an open country. This great tract of country, extending from Winnipeg to Stony Mountain, is a portion of the Halfbreed reservation, and will of necessity remain unsettled for years, unless placed into the hands of trustees, the lands sold, and the proceeds invested for the minors interested. The following morning we were invited by Dr. Schultz to take a drive to the Stone Fort, commonly called Lower Fort Garry, distant from Winnipeg, down the Red River, 20 miles. The roads being good, the Doctor's spanking team soon brought us into the Scotch Settlement of Kildonan, probably the most fertile and best settled portion of the Province. Only a small strip bordering on the river, in many places not exceeding a mile in width, has been brought under cultivation, which has been cropped for nearly half a century, and yet yields abundant crops with very indifferent cultivation.

THE HIGHLANDERS OF MANITOBA.

The descendants of those hardy Highland veterans who were mercilessly driven from the estate of a former Duchess of Sutherland, the roofs torn from their dwellings, and ejected from the homes of their fathers, found shelter ultimately in these remote regions, 1,500 miles from any civilized community, among cruel and untutored savages. Many where killed by the Indians or servants of rival companies, and many died of hunger and starvation. Those old pioncers have, with but few exceptions, passed away. Many of their offspring have Indian blood flowing through their veins, and are not as rugged and cannot endure the privations and hardships which their fathers had to undergo. Many are wealthy, mostly all in comfortable circumstances. A general sentiment of benevolence unites every family. They preserve with prejudice the Gaelic language and seem to possess mutual attachment. No race of people are more attachedo each other than the Highlanders of Manitoba. Their lands are of unbounded fertility, composed of alluvial deposits, and have borne uninterrupted tillage for nearly half a century, without using any artificial means. Many are agricultural Pharisees, who cling with great tenacity to the old exploded notions and traditions of their forefathers. Perpetual tillage and no rotation of crops must depreciate the soil. Each species of grain takes from the land specific food or particles, which other species do not. Some returns must be made in the shape of manure, seeding down or change of crops, or the lands become impoverished. Scores of these Highlanders carted their barn manures into the river, until the Legislature were under the necessity of passing an act to prevent them. Now many evade the law by carting the manure on the river banks, and the spring floods carry it away. The farms are very inconvenient, being narrow strips, having a frontage of six or eight chains on the river and running to the rear two miles, with an additional two miles of meadow lands still further to the rear.

The absence of ornamental trees in the clearings or around the farm buildings certainly shows a want of taste. The sugar maple may grow, but I saw none in the Province; but poplar, willow, spruce, elm, and oak will grow very rapidly, and add very materially to the appearance of the farm. Some assert that the loose, friable nature of the soil, combined with an excess of alkaline or saline constituents in its composition, accounts for the scanty growth of timber. I have noticed some fruit trees that had a withered, sickly appearance, but no care is taken of them. In the woods we find that wild fruit trees grow and produce largely. I have heard some complaining who are not acquainted with the climate, of the dryness of the atmosphere and the absence of refreshing showers in summer, and that such drought would retard the growth of crops. Such, however, is not the case. The frost in winter penetrates to a great depth and the earth retains its moisture; the heat of summer raises this moisture, which evaporates unperceived during the day. It also rises at night and falls or lies upon the land in copious dews, quite sufficient for the growth of plants. What these Kildonan men require, is a few good, scientific, practical farmers planted among them. They would then soon imitate their example, and their old exploded notions of husbandry would speedily disappear. On our way we pass St. John's church. We notice two old windmills that answered their purpose years gone by, but are now allowed to decay. A few miles further we pass the

SCOTCH CHURCH OF REV. MR. BLACK.

This devoted minister has labored for a quarter of a century among his flock, and is very popular with his people. Passing St. Paul's English church, we enter poplar groves and woodland for a few miles, and reach the Fort, which is situated near the banks of the river. Many excellent and comfortable buildings are in this locality and considerable land is under cultivation. The Hudson Bay Company owns 500 acres adjoining the Fort. Present indication and current rumors are that the great Pacific Railway will cross the Red river at the fort, or between the fort and the rapids. (One of the principal engineers, Mr. Rowan, was during my visit surveying in that locality.) If so, the property of the company will become very valuable, and this great monopoly under Imperial authority will realize another fortune out of the bungling of the late Ottawa Administration. The fort is built of limestone, quarried in the immediate locality, and pierced with numerous loop holes. The premises are large, and to all appearance, particularly during the summer months, the season of navigation, an enormous trade is carried on. After viewing the store, officers' quarters, grist mill, &c., we were invited by the Governor of the jail, Mr. Bedson, to examine his extensive gardans and the interior of the prison. The garden covers an area of between two and three acres, laid out with excellent taste, expense and labor, and is decidedly the best garden I ever saw in connection with such institutions, but the grasshoppers had taken possession and had made sad havoc of the vegetables and fancy flower beds. We noticed two bears in one corner of the garden wrestling in a playful manner. The interior of the jail is kept scrupulously clean and orderly. The prisoners were all at work in gangs of three or four. Many suspicious, hardened characters had a ball and chain dragging after them. Among the convicts were a few Indians with their heads shaved, which must to a native be in itself the greatest degradation. Leaving the fort we took a pleasant drive up the river road, and in half an hour we arrive at Dr. Schultz's residence, a charming location overlooking the river, which is wide in that neighborhood, with high banks and a rapid current. The doctor seems to flourish like a "green bay tree," surrounded with all the elements of comfort (except those little prattlers which usually add a charm to domestic life.) In the society of Dr. Schultz and his kind, amiable partner, we passed an hour or two very enjoyably, and proceeded on our return to Winnipeg. Before we reached Kildonan we were overtaken by a dreadful thunder storm that had been gathering for some hours. The lightning was intensly vivid and the thunder terrific. Our hardy equines were driven by the violence of the storm to the fence, entirely out of the beaten track, and remained immovable with their backs to the storm till its fury had abated. We were all literally drenched to the skin. In half an hour the road was a perfect sea of water, and to our astonishment when we arrived at Winnipeg, distant only three miles, our account of the storm was scarcely credited, a drizzling rain only having passed over the city.

Next week we will resume our ramblings through other sections of Manitoba.

Yours truly,

JAMES TROW.

DEAR SIR,—I was anxious to keep myself engaged daily during my limited stay in the Province in visiting the various settlements, and accordingly the following morning after our excursion to the Stone Fort, we made arrangements to drive to Springfield and Sunnyside, two Canadian settlements ten or twelve miles north-east from Winnipeg. Mr. McVicar, formerly a resident of Kent, Ontario, now in company with his sons carrying on an extensive woollen manufactory in Winnipeg, volunteered to drive us out.

Crossing the Red River, we found the water low, the banks high and the approaches nearly in their natural state, at an angle of forty-five degrees to the water's edge. During low water the passage across is tedious. The ferry is driven by the current.

A MANITOBA GRIEVANCE.

While seated comfortably in the buggy, we were accosted by our companion in the following style: " Why," he asked, " can we have any sympathy for the Dominion Government, when they lack enterprise ? How long are we to be kept isolated from the older Provinces ? We are entirely British, and wish to cling to British connection, but we are separated through necessity ; we have no communication excepting through the States to the other Provinces. The Americans are enterprising and sociable, but they take advantage of our situation, and simply because we are a portion of the Dominion, we are obliged to pay a discriminating tariff for freight, amounting to nearly 300 per cent. more than those who purchase goods in the United States. During low water, rates are raised from $3 to $3.50 per 100 lbs. from St. Paul, and they would be much higher were it not for competition with owners of flat-bottom boats, who carry enormous quantities of goods and after they arrive, take their boats to pieces and sell the lumber. A bridge spanning the river at this point was promised by the late Administration and also by those now in power, and the necessary sums put on the estimates. Why should it be witheld ? My own expenses, crossing and recrossing, average at least one dollar per day." By this time we had made the opposite bank, and in driving up the steep grade, my friend nearly lost his balance. This little accident gave me a favorable opportunity to turn the argument against him by remarking that "the smallest petty corporation in Ontario would not allow those approaches to remain in that state twenty-four hours without repairs; that a pathmaster alone, providing the municipality neglected to provide for the improvement, would do so himself, and not run the risk of being prosecuted for allowing the roads in his division to become impassable. Yet here within the city limits, the main leading thoroughfare is almost impassable, when the expenditure of fifty dollars would, make a good road. You require to be thrown upon your own resources, and unless you show a spirit of enterprise yourselves, how can you expect assistance from abroad?"

Ascending the plateau, or church reservation, in the Parish of St. Boniface, we intended paying a visit to

ARCHBISHOP TACHÉ,

but were informed that His Lordship was absent on a tour, visiting his flock. We casually examined the exterior of the cathedral, the Archiepiscopal palace, school convents and pleasure grounds, which amply repay a visit. They are situated at the confluence of the Assiniboine with the Red River, on the opposite bank from the town and fort. Some of the buildings are of stone and very substantial. The old cathedral was destroyed by fire during the absence of Bishop Taché to the Saskatchewan in 1860. The Bishop took a tour afterwards to France, Rome and other parts of the continent and succeeded in obtaining funds to erect the present structure. Dr. Taché first settled in the North West in 1845, and travelled in the interior as a missionary till the death of Bishop Provencher, when he was appointed his successor. The members of his church are principally French half-breeds, but scores of other nationalities regularly attend service. He is exceedingly popular with all classes of the community. The church property embraces nearly a township on the Red River and Seine. A large portion is under very indifferent cultivation.

A PROSPEROUS SETTLEMENT.

Proceeding on our way, through numerous poplar groves, for three or four miles, we emerge into the open prairie extending on the east to Oak Point, and on the north to a range of elevations above the surrounding country, covered with oak, elm, and poplar, called the Springfield settlement. Arriving at the settlement we were entertained by Captain McDougall. After examining the various formations comprising these moderate sized hills, we follow the windings of the road along the top of the ridge to Sunnyside, were we found many Canadians surrounded with all the elements of comfort. Many were busily engaged cutting the wheat crop, which was not seriously injured. The oat crop was destroyed. The staple crop is wheat. Where land will produce from 25 to 35 bushels of good wheat to the acre and potatoes, turnips, onions, and all other vegetables in the greatest profusion, and any quantity of hay, farmers have certainly no reason to complain. To a stranger the little log dwellings have a shabby and desolate appearance ; indeed I was much surprised to find that persons in possession of ample means did not display more taste. The house are generally made of short logs or poles, both ends fastened into grooves made into upright logs, from the sills to the beam. These squares are filled up, and when finished the walls are plastered with mud and whitewashed, the door and window forming one of the squares. The roofs are covered with poles close together and thatched with long prairie grass, puddled with mud. Their exterior is not attractive, but comfort often reigns within. Many of the farmers are somewhat discouraged at the ravages of the grasshoppers, but have every hope that the plague will be of short duration. Otherwise they are well satisfied with the country. The prairies are a very inviting place for a home. Nature has made all the requisite preparation, no trees, stumps or stones to clear, nothing to do but commence ploughing. To hew and clear up a farm in Ontario, is a life-consuming task, even for a Canadian who is accustomed to wield the axe; the first settlers are completely broken down before the stumps are eradicated. The struggle is doubly hard for an immigrant who is not accustomed to such work. In Manitoba young boys can manage the plough. It is a pleasure to till the soil and not a hardship, and the wear and tear of implements is not nearly so great as on timber lands. After a pleasant drive of probably thirty or forty miles, we returned late at night to the city.

The following day, in company with Mr. John Grant, surveyor, we drove to the parish of St. Norbert, to Sale or Stinking River. The river lots are mostly all under partial cultivation, many farmers having large clearings extending from the Red River. The buildings are principally near the river banks. This section is thickly settled with French half-breeds on both sides of the river. Many devote more time to hunting and trading than they do to agriculture. Scores are very anxious to dispose of their property and remove further inland.

A GENERAL OPINION OF THE COUNTRY.

After travelling for four weeks through the settled portions of the Province, I am fully convinced that no portion of Her Majesty's Dominion is better calculated for agricultural purposes, than the Province of Manitoba. It abounds in plants of every description, from the pine to the smallest shrub. It is true a large portion of the land is destitute of trees, but where protected they grow rapidly. The coal regions west may yet make up for the scarcity of timber. The province is rich in salt, of which indications are seen in many parts, salt licks and alkaline patches are frequently met with. Wood is purchased at Winnipeg at $2.75 and $3 per cord, and good lumber from $20 to $25 per 1000 feet. A free grant of 160 acres is made to any person over 18 years of age, on condition of three years' settlement, and the settler may obtain 160 acres additional on three years' credit at $1 per acre. Timber lands are disposed of so as to benefit the greatest possible number of settlers. The price of wheat ranges from $1.25 to $1.35, barley the same; oats, $1; potatoes from 50 to 75 cts. per bushel; onions $2; beef $12\frac{1}{2}$ cts.; pork 18 to 20 cts.; butter 30 to 35 cts.; board at hotels from $6 to $9 per week. Rents are enormously high. Every building is occupied, but men of capital will soon see the propriety of erecting buildings for mechanics and laboring men. Wages range for mechanics from $2.50 to $3.50 per day; laboring men $1.50 to $2; servant girls from $15 to $20 per month. The weather is delightful in summer; the middle of the day is warm, but the nights and mornings are refreshing and cool. I am informed that the winters are not longer or more severe than in Ontario, and much shorter and even milder than in Quebec or New Brunswick. The depth of snow scarcely ever exceeds 18 inches, and there are no storms, rains, or thaws. The atmosphere is very pure and the weather uniform. Winter sets in generally about the middle of November, and Spring opens early in April, when vegetation shoots up very rapidly. The rural districts are healthy. No one experiences depression of spirits or want of animal vigor. Some persons are subject to fevers in Winnipeg, this season particularly, owing to excessive droughts. The sewerage being very defective, the accumulation of filth produces foul air ; poisonous gases mix and pollute the atmosphere.

THE PRESS OF WINNIPEG

will compare favorably with that of any town or city of similar size, there being five weekly and two daily papers, which are very creditably conducted, though occasionally they get wonderfully irritated and feverish against one another. Free discussion is largely tolerated, but notwithstanding, I am informed the best of friendship exists. The inhabitants are noted for sobriety, very few indulge to excess, yet some traders, after months of absence, like seamen after a long voyage, do at times exceed the bounds of moderation and prefer the music of the popping of corks to the roar of a cataract. A large proportion of the Province is yet unsettled. Small settlements are scattered here and there, and new settlements are made every year. Very little means of communication at present throughout the country. It is essential that means of communication should at once be made, leading arteries should be opened, and the most distant parts should be made more accessible by a system of good roads. This can easily be accomplished without pressure upon the resources of the Dominion. The

Province having no adequate resources of its own, is dependent upon the general Government for the construction of public works. The Pembina line" extending from the boundary to Winnipeg, is now in course of construction. When that banch is completed and the American portion finished to Pembina, the colonist will have greater facilities for the transportation of goods and rapid communication with other portions of the Dominion. The rapid increase of trade demands imperatively the immediate construction of railroads. The amount of imports for the fiscal year ending 30th June, 1872, according to official reports were—from Great Britain, $655,189; Ontario and Quebec, only $16,919; United States, $321,658; other countries, $26,406. Total imports, $1,820,172; amount of duty received, $46,830.90. Most likely the imports for 1874 would exceed those of 1872, by at least 50 per cent.

Before leaving the Province we spent a very pleasant evening at the Government House, with Governor Morris and family. The Hon. Mr. Laird, Hon. E. B. Wood, Hon. Mr. Norquay, Mr. Howard and several other gentlemen were present. Governor Morris is certainly a man of the world, natural without affectation, and exceedingly social.

HOMEWARD BOUND.

The following evening we took passage on board the steamer *Dakota* for Moorhead, distant, according to Captain Painter's calculation, 550 miles by water; by stage route 250 miles. We steamed around the numerous windings of the river, cut through deep alluvial rich soil, the banks fringed with reeds and rank undergrowth, from which at almost every bend a covey of ducks or other water fowl would skim before the boat. Late in the evening we came in sight of the residence of the Hon. Joseph Royal, late Provincial Secretary. Our boat is hailed and Mr. Royal and daughters come on board, bound for Montreal. Steaming up the Red River is the most monotonous travelling imaginable. The river banks are high at low water, hemmed in by tall poplars, and the scenery much the same from day to day. You are sailing in a large deep ditch and can chew the cud of your reflections at your leisure. There is nothing to annoy you in the cabin excepting innumerable mosquitoes and black flies, and no annoyance on deck unless a few sparks from the smoke pipe occasionally burning a hole in your coat. About 2 o'clock on the second morning of our voyage we arrive at Pembina, the dividing line between the Province of Manitoba and the United States. The Fort is on the Dakota side of the river. The Hudson Bay Company have a trading establishment on the other side. You are unceremoniously awakened from your slumbers, and requested to hand over your keys to the custom house officer, who unceremoniously overhauls your baggage. No contraband goods were found with any of the passengers. The odor arising from a few pounds of pemmican in my trunk for distribution among my friends, probably prevented my clothing being disarranged. We are now in the Great American Republic. I may in future letters continue my ramblings through the United States.

Yours truly,

JAMES TROW.

www.ingramcontent.com/pod-product-compliance
Lightning Source LLC
Chambersburg PA
CBHW020307090426
42735CB00009B/1252